Paths of the Western Sun
Volume I

Modern pictograph atop Pilot Rock

Mahmoud Shelton

Ancient Secrets
of the
Rogue Valley

Temple of Justice Books

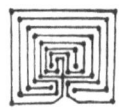

Copyright © 2022 D.M. Shelton

All rights reserved. This book or any portion thereof may not be reproduced or used in any manner whatsoever without the express written permission of the publisher.

templeofjustice@icloud.com

Printed in the United States of America

ISBN
978-0-9741468-5-0

Cover and diagrams by C.M. Design

But Eden is burning
Either get ready for elimination
Or else your hearts must have courage
For the changing of the guards.

Bob Dylan

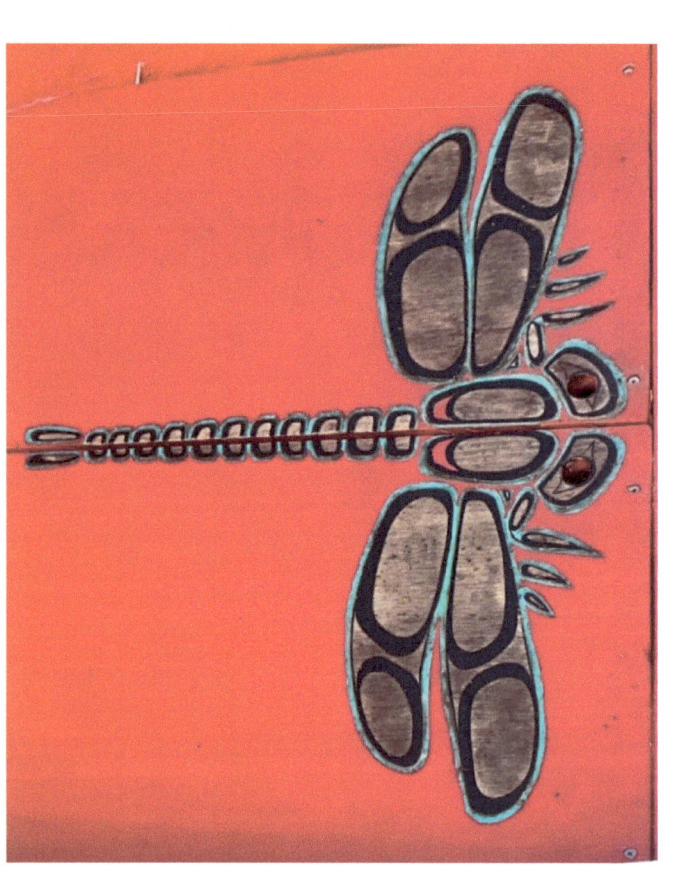

Contents

1	Forgotten but not Gone	9
2	The Cascade-Siskiyou Knot	23
3	Waters of Life and Death	37
4	Sermons in Stones	51
5	The Solar Ray	69
6	That Which is Lost	83
7	The Morning Star	95

View of the Rogue Valley from the Table Rocks

1

Forgotten but not Gone

The 42nd parallel marks a historic borderline of sorts between Spanish and British interests in the Americas, and this line remains the border between the modern states of California and Oregon, among others.[1] California's Mount Shasta, the sacred mountain of Native tradition, rises to the south of this border, while immediately to its north is found Southern Oregon's greatest concentration of towns in an area called the Rogue Valley. The region marks more than political divides, since the valley lies between the ancient Siskiyou mountain range to the west and the active volcanic Cascade Range to the east. The place still retains something of its primordial appearance, having been largely spared the excesses of urban development. Even so, the Rogue Valley is widely known in the West due to its position along the principal travel corridor between North and South, a corridor that generally follows more ancient paths through the mountain valleys. Many tourists visit annually to enjoy the Oregon Shakespeare Festival, which to a greater or lesser

---

[1] On the cultural significance of the 42nd parallel, see "The Modocs and a World's Heart," *Guardians of the Heart: Essays on Sacred Geography,* Temple of Justice Books, 2022, page 33.

degree provides insights into Western culture and history, yet neither locals nor tourists are very familiar with the challenging history of the Rogue Valley. Many are drawn to the Rogue River itself, with ecotourism offering ways for modern people to enjoy the river's "Wild and Scenic" character without any deeper context. However, even the river's name is a reference to its traditional peoples. "Rogue" is in fact a translation of the French word *coquin*, a derogatory name applied to them by French fur trappers who are presumed to have been the first Europeans to reach the river. The name remains, yet the rupture with ancient tradition that was signaled by the arrival of Europeans occurred not only with alarming rapidity here, but by means of a total genocide.

The first recorded contact between the Natives of the Rogue Valley with the agents of the Hudson Bay Company was in 1826 or 1827. By the end of the Rogue River Wars of 1855-6, all traditional life from the Rogue Valley was destroyed or removed after having been sustained for millennia. Violence against the Native peoples began as early as 1834. By 1846, much greater numbers were immigrating to the Rogue Valley after the Applegate Trail[2] provided an alternative route through the Cascade Mountains. Like for so many other places in the Far West, the Gold Rush brought economic opportunity at the expense of ecological sense, and a disproportionate burden of immigrants unaccompanied by families. Of course, with these developments the Native populations were increasingly under threat; but the case of the Rogue Valley presents an extreme example of how the invaders found a "final solution" to the challenges presented by the very existence of the myriad communities that were

---

[2] This section of the Applegate Trail was named for Jesse Applegate; on his complicity in the causes of the Modoc Wars see "The Modocs and a World's Heart," op. cit.

grouped together as "Rogue River Indians." Native people were systematically hunted and killed by volunteer militias. Under these conditions, the American military played a relatively minor role, although it oversaw the brief existence of a reservation along the river at a place known as the Table Rocks. Nevertheless, the Rogue River Wars of 1855-6 brought a swift end to traditional life in the Rogue Valley. All surviving Native people were force-marched to reservations in the distant North. Over time, the Rogue River Indians became assimilated primarily with the Siletz people of the Coast, and their knowledge of the landscape of the Rogue Valley would necessarily recede into distant memory.

According to a tradition of the Takelma or "River People" that was recorded,[3] the two mesas called the Table Rocks are at the center of the Rogue River's extent. The Takelma perceived their homeland as corresponding to a great "beast," with the river as its life "blood." The Table Rocks were understood to be its "ribs."[4] The "head" and "neck" of the beast were associated with the Crater Lake area in the rugged heights of the volcanic Cascade Mountains; from its "ribs," the life currents of the river descended through the steep canyons of the Siskiyou Mountains towards the Pacific and its "tail." The centrality of the Table Rocks was even formerly recognized by the immigrants in their own manner. After the Rogue River Wars, an attempt was made to establish a capital town of sorts at the

---

[3] Cf. "Ribs of the Animal" in Thomas Doty, *Doty Meets Coyote*, Ashland: Blackstone Publishing, 2016. In the wake of genocide, efforts were made, notably by the heroic ethnographer John P. Harrington, to record Native lore from the surviving individuals who preserved it.

[4] There was formerly a mysterious deep pit atop Lower Table Rock, but its circular opening was closed off in recent years to protect the public.

confluence of Bear Creek with the Rogue River in the shadow of the Table Rocks. This town was named Tolo,[5] though nothing remains of the failed settlement now. Significantly, the nearest town to its former position is called simply "Central Point." Tolo was not to be the only failure inflicted upon this confluence of waterways. Not long after the turning of the 20th century, the Gold Ray hydroelectric dam was built just downstream. At least the ecological harm inflicted by this folly would eventually be undone, since the dam was in fact removed in 2010.

In keeping with the centrality of the Table Rocks for the Rogue River, there is a centrality to Bear Creek in relation to the Rogue Valley. Although the valley of Bear Creek is now considered synonymous with the Rogue Valley, this is geographically imprecise. Regardless, the Applegate Trail took advantage of the open landscape formed by the intersection of the two watercourses.[6] While the Rogue Valley is formed by the river's course from the Cascade to the Siskiyou Mountains, the separation of these ranges is even more explicitly defined by Bear Creek. This creek was in fact formerly called the Stuart River, and so its status has been somewhat downgraded over time; yet the Rogue Valley as it is presently understood corresponds to the orientation of its course that flows from southeast to northwest. The principal towns of the Rogue Valley – including Ashland, Talent, Phoenix, Medford, and Central Point – are located not

---

[5] While its etymology is supposedly traced to a spelling error or to Chinook jargon, its similarity to the names Tula or Thule for a spiritual center should not be overlooked (cf. *The Red and the White: Perspectives on America and the Primordial Tradition*, Temple of Justice Books, 2019, page 18). The name Talent for another Rogue Valley town continues to echo the name Tolo.

[6] Unlike the Columbia River that was followed by the Oregon Trail, the course of the Rogue River did not provide an opening for immigrants to pass through the Cascades.

The confluence of Bear Creek and the Rogue River
under the horseshoe-shaped Table Rocks

upon the Rogue River, but upon the Rogue Valley's central "axis" of Bear Creek.

There are, moreover, special characteristics of the Bear Valley that distinguish it from the greater Rogue Valley, especially in its upper reaches. The academic question of whether Upper Bear Creek should be included in the traditional territory of the Takelma has never been resolved. The town plaza of Ashland occupies the place of a village more certainly associated with the Shasta people. The name of the Ashland region, with its community focus at the village, seems to have been *K'wakhakha*, "Where the Crow

Lights."[7] Three distinct bands of the Shasta were situated in Northern California, but a fourth band was apparently found in the Bear Creek watershed by the first American immigrants. "The northern extent of Shastan territory is a matter of uncertainty. It has sometimes been claimed to include considerable area on the Rogue River watershed, and at other times to extend only to the summit of the Siskiyous."[8] For the ethnographer Edward Sapir, the Rogue River watershed was a disputed territory between the Takelma and Shasta. More specifically, a separate group of the Takelma, the so-called Latgawa or "Upland Takelma," should be recognized as the natural rivals of the Shasta in the highlands away from the Rogue, where less sedentary patterns of life would be practiced. To make matters worse, the northern band of Shasta were by no means allied with the other bands, making a united response to invasion unlikely.

Beyond these historical considerations, it is important to recognize that there is evidence in support of a very long Native presence in the environs of Ashland, compared to which the last two centuries represent a period of insignificant duration. In a recent inventory of all discovered Clovis points[9] from a wider area including Northern California, Southern Oregon, and Eastern Nevada, the greatest concentration has been found in and around

---

[7] Nan Hannon, "Tipsu Tyee: Last Chief of the Ashland Creek People," *Southern Oregon Heritage Today*, volume 3 number 10, Medford: Southern Oregon Historical Society.

[8] Joel V. Berreman, "Tribal Distribution in Oregon," *Memoirs of the American Anthropological Association*, number 47, Menasha, 1937, page 26. Adding to the obscurity on this matter, perhaps, is the fact that the Shasta people remain unrecognized by the United States government.

[9] The so-called Clovis Point is the head of a thrown weapon with distinctive characteristics that has been dated to more than 10000 years before the present.

Ashland.[10] This places the prehistory of the Bear Creek drainage in the Paleoindian period, and so evaluating the area as a disputed tribal territory must consider more than the historic presence of the Shasta and Takelma.

With the development of Ashland at the head of the Bear Valley, another specialty of the place came to be recognized that no doubt had played an important role in the region's prehistory:

> Every one (*sic*) who knows anything about southern Oregon, especially the southernmost end of the Rogue River valley, knows that medicinal springs abound in this region. There are Hellman Sulphur Springs, Jackson Hot Sulphur Springs, Tolman Springs, Wagner Soda Springs, Colestin Springs, Ashland Mineral Springs, Ashland Lithia Springs, Shepherd's Soda Springs and Kingsbury's Soda Springs and a score or more others which have not been dignified as yet with names.[11]

At present, it would seem that hardly anyone "knows anything about southern Oregon," since this truly special abundance and variety is all but ignored. Ancient people must have known what modern people do not concerning these springs, and there is evidence of Native use of at least two of them. "Jackson Hot Sulphur Springs" was traditionally known as a "Poison Lake," though the lake has

---

[10] Jack Meyer, "A Geoarchaeological Overview and Assessment of Northeast California," Cultural Resources Inventory of Caltrans District 2, Redding, 2013, page 125.

[11] Emerson Holt, "Building a City on Health," *Sunset Magazine*, volume 34, number 2, February 1915.

been drained.¹² As for the term "poison," we must keep in mind that the unseen *genii loci* of certain places were traditionally regarded as being a source both of healing and of sickness, and their dangerous character was indicated by the Shasta name for them: *axaiki*, or "pain."¹³ Another site

Jackson Hot Springs
before the "poison lake" was drained

---

¹² These spring waters are still used privately by some and made available to the public at Jackson Wellsprings and Lithia Springs Resort; the name of the latter is confusing since the waters are not from a Lithia spring.

¹³ On the universal belief in these beings throughout Native America, see John Roth's *American Elves* (Jefferson: McFarland, 1997); on page 67, reference is made to the Shasta belief: "Pains reside near or in rocks, cliffs, mountains, lakes, peaks, rapids, eddies…Ancient artifacts indicate where they live…The most magic or powerful ones lived near Rogue River."

now known as Buckhorn Springs has long been associated with Native use. As recently as the 1970s, two "crescent-shaped mounds" preserved at the site were offered as proof of a Native presence there.[14] Curiously, Buckhorn Springs was originally called "Poison Water" by immigrants, no doubt due to its noxious vapors, but it is not clear if this designation followed a Native precedent.

In the early 20th century, the city of Ashland was taking steps towards becoming a spa town after the European model. Its hopes were focused especially on its Lithia soda water, which was determined to have the strongest Lithium content after a spring in Karlovy Vary, the greatest of Europe's spa towns better known as Carlsbad. It was not without reason that Ashland advertised a claim to be the "Carlsbad of America." The source of the Lithia Water was at that time the so-called "Pompadour Chief" spring located some three miles from the plaza. Even though the location of its source was developed as a park, the decision was soon made to pipe its waters to various locations around the city. Lithia Park was developed to complement the healing power in the water, with the former being named for the latter. The realization of the spa town would go no further, however, following the upheavals of the First World War. Most but not all of the Lithia fountains around the town were eventually removed; the thermal spring that supplied the water for the city's natatorium would eventually be covered over by a parking lot.[15] Of the more than fifty springs once celebrated in the area, almost all "are either closed to the public or fallen into total oblivion."[16]

---

[14] Howard Horowitz, "The Landscapes of Hot Springs and Mineral Springs in Western Oregon," University of Oregon thesis, 1973.
[15] A Japanese-style bathhouse presently operates down the street from the abandoned hot spring by heating tap water.
[16] Ibid., page 84.

To understand the import of these observations, we would do well to return to John Michell's remarks on the European invasion of America:

> Until recently, every migrating race inherited from the native magicians of the new country the spiritual secrets of the landscape, respecting the superior knowledge and experience of the former people in natural magic, and even, in the course of time, coming to identify their memory with the local spirits, elementals, and *genii loci*. The European colonists in America were, perhaps, the first to exterminate the native inhabitants without learning the secrets of their geomancy, of the seasons proper for invoking the fertilizing influences and of the sacred spots appropriate for that purpose.[17]

In the case of Ashland, it could hardly be supposed that the choice of locating the plaza upon the site of the Native village was based upon geomantic considerations. However, the use of the springs of the Upper Bear Creek Valley does suggest

---

[17] *The New View Over Atlantis*, San Francisco: Harper & Row, 1983, page 199. By "geomancy," the reader should understand not the `ilm ul-raml` of the Islamic world – the Medieval source of the English word, by way of Latin – but rather a cosmological science akin to the Feng Shui that was familiar to Michell.

an important comparison. Just as the knowledge of medicinal springs belonged to Native tradition, the settlers' use of the springs represents a last vestige of an ancient European tradition, perpetuated under the auspices of the Roman Empire.[18] Indeed, if the teachings of Pythagoras and Plato should be identified with the Apollonian tradition, as I have explained elsewhere, then the very foundations of European thinking should be traced to the Delphic Apollo and the springs of Mount Parnassus.[19] The hope of modelling Ashland after the spas of Europe was far more than a passing fancy.

Respect for healing springs may indeed be universal, yet both Natives and settlers in Ashland specifically knew that "poison" was also present in the waters of healing. Even if poorly understood, this reality relates to the *genius loci* or unseen aspect unique to each place. The name "Pompadour Chief" may seem to be an example of cultural appropriation, but perhaps it serves to acknowledge an authority related to the foremost cliff in the vicinity, Pompadour Bluff. Regardless, the decision to pipe the Lithia waters away from their source denies the role of the *genius loci*.[20] As for the

---

[18] Examples of Celtic sanctuaries taken over by the Romans are legion, even as far as Bath in England. Carlsbad is named for Charles IV, the first King of Bohemia to become Holy Roman Emperor. It is somehow appropriate that the First World War signaled the end of Ashland's hopes to become a spa town, since it also brought the end of the Holy Roman Empire in both the Ottoman East and Habsburg West.

[19] On the Apollonian tradition, see *Sacred Geography and the Paths of the Sun* (Temple of Justice Books, 2021).

[20] There was initially a widespread debate concerning whether bottled soda waters contained the same healing virtues as those taken directly at the source, but this debate failed to consider the role of the *genius loci*. This failure would lead to the establishing of counterfeit "soda fountains" in pharmacies, a popular 20th century

A forgotten sulphur spring

place of this source, the park land has since been taken over by a gun and archery club, and it would be hard to imagine any more wasted condition for the site than its present one, with no access there to the medicinal water.[21]

---

practice. Curiously, the etymology of the word "pharmacy" includes the notion of poison, and modern people would do well to at least recognize the dangers of pharmaceuticals. As for modern sodas, these parodies of healing waters came to be an identifiable cause of a health crisis in the late 20th century, especially among young people, in large measure through the addition of corn syrup that artificially derives from the sacred plant of Native civilization.
[21] The waters of a sulphur spring were at one time likewise piped into Lithia Park from a distant place (labelled point 5 on page 30), and it is worth noting that the artificial cave where they were made

Forgotten but not Gone

The shared use of mineral springs in the Upper Bear Creek Valley provides a glimpse of a theme so essential to my study *The Red and the White*. For many Native peoples, the invasion of Europeans signaled the possible return of an "ancient white people" whose customs were in harmony with their own. While the tragic irony of this hope is all too clear in retrospect, it is worth recalling, for example, that when the Hopi were evaluating whether the Spanish might be their lost brothers, it was the violence of the Spanish that revealed a nature quite contrary to the peacefulness of their ancient brethren.[22] It would be difficult to find a region that witnessed more terrible violence against Native populations than the setting of the Rogue River Wars. Thankfully those times are gone, but so are the indigenous peoples from these lands, excepting the few from various tribes who have chosen to return to the region. To add insult to injury, as it were, the falling of the mineral springs into "oblivion" – a word that means to be "forgotten" – proves that the less violent residents now living in the Rogue Valley care less for the native springs than those closer to genocide.[23] If there is yet hope to address the errors of the past, it is not through forgetfulness. Even now, and despite neglect, the spring waters of the Rogue Valley still bubble to the surface; stones

---

available was designated "Satan's Grotto" in the absence of the actual *genius loci*. The structure at its source (previous page) has been lost through neglect, whereas nothing at all remains of Satan's Grotto, since it was completely destroyed by floodwaters in the early 1970s.

[22] Cf. *The Red and the White*, op. cit., page 80. It has been reported that below the plaza and above Bear Creek, there had been a field for the resolution of conflict through a tradition of stylized combat (see Hannon, op. cit.)

[23] Even though Lithia Water continues to be piped into Ashland, it seems to be regarded rather as a joke for tourists than a resource for healing.

of ancient memory yet remain on the landscape; and the crows still fly over Ashland, even if so few remember the Native name that acknowledges them.[24]

---

[24] "Ashland" has no apparent local relevance, being a name transplanted ultimately from a plantation in Kentucky where slave laborers harvested hemp. In recent years, the growing of hemp has been legalized in Oregon and is a factor in the local economy, and its burden on reduced water resources is considerable.

2

The Cascade-Siskiyou Knot

Native lore regarding the ancient white people is associated with a renewal that followed a cataclysmic flood, and indeed many Native traditions are formulated in relation to this renewal. For example, the Hopi account of the Bahana or "white brother" involves a separation from him that came after the flood. Of course, the Great Flood is a familiar theme in mythology, and I have explained elsewhere that the postdiluvian world witnessed the emergence of so many traditional forms that are easily compared since they arose out of comparable conditions; even the Classical world was able to identify in the Egyptian tradition, for example, the same figures venerated in their own.[25] In the Abrahamic traditions, the dispersal of the three sons of Noah gave rise to the various races of the Earth. For the Shasta people of Native America, there are three mountains that were not submerged by the flood, and so these are points that may be understood to define the world that emerged after: "Mount Shasta, another mountain near

---

[25] On the lore relating to the Bahana, see *The Red and the White*, as well as for a consideration of these comparable traditional forms and why Native tradition must be included among them.

Happy Camp called Old Man Mountain, and another at the head of Rogue River."[26]

Legends of a flood likewise belong to the Chinese tradition, and we have had occasion before to compare the lore of China with that of the Shasta people in particular. In *The Red and the White*, the clear equivalence between the Shasta legend of Coyote slaying the Sun's nine brothers and the Chinese legend of Yi the Archer shooting down nine monstrous suns was noted for the first time. What makes this equivalence especially important is that the setting of the Oriental legend is the mythical land of Fusang far to the east of China; and Fusang has long been suspected to be the American West, that is, the land that includes the home of the Shasta.[27] Fusang, however, belongs to a larger mythic geography of the Eastern Sea that includes sometimes five, but originally three, mountain isles of the Taoist Immortals. Inasmuch as these mountain isles of Penglai, Fangzhang, and Yangzhou represent a perennial existence, they may easily be compared with the three mountains of the Shasta that remained unchanged through the flood, especially in the context of a growing body of evidence that indicates a Chinese presence in ancient Native America.[28]

As for the mountains of the Shasta, only Mount Shasta is found on modern maps, yet there are sufficient clues to clarify the identity of the other two. Towering above all other peaks near Happy Camp is Preston Peak, and so this height is recognized easily enough as Old Man Mountain. The remaining mountain is not named, but its location betrays its identity. However, this identification may seem unlikely for a teaching handed down in historic times, since

---

[26] Catharine Holt, "Shasta Ethnography," *Anthropological Records* 3:4, Berkeley: University of California Press, 1946, page 326.

[27] *The Red and the White.*, chapter 7.

[28] See Ibid. and "The Modocs and a World's Heart."

the mountain with which it must be identified has not existed for some 7000 years.[29] Geologists call the peak Mount Mazama, and Crater Lake is presumed to be what was left after the volcanic destruction of a very great mountain indeed. We have already observed that for the Takelma, Crater Lake was quite literally the "head" of the Rogue River. As for the likelihood of the Shasta describing a landscape more than 7000 years old, this should not be too surprising, since the flood is older still; and in the case of Crater Lake, academics have come to admit that Native legends preserve a remarkably accurate memory of the destruction of Mount Mazama.[30] Specifically, these legends associate Crater Lake with Llao, lord of the Underworld,[31] whose rival is Skell, and Skell is considered to be a form of Gmukamps who is often enough associated with Mount Shasta and a corresponding Sky Lodge.[32]

---

[29] The "non-existence" of the mountain may very well account for the fact that of the three peaks, this is the only one without a proper name. For his part, local authority Jeffrey LaLande (*Prehistory and History of the Rogue River National Forest: A Cultural Resource Overview*, Medford, 1980, page 123) assumes this third peak to be Mount Mcloughlin; but the Shasta do have a name for this peak, and even more importantly, McLoughlin is simply not at the head of the Rogue River.

[30] Cf. Douglas Deur, *In the Footsteps of Gmukamps: A Traditional Use Study of Crater Lake National Monument and Lava Beds National Monument*, National Park Service, 2008, pages 55-61.

[31] Wizard Island in Crater Lake is considered to be the severed head of Llao, and this even more explicitly recalls the Takelma description of the great beast of the world.

[32] This distinction is worth comparing with the "Three Steps of Vishnu" of Hindu cosmogony that relate to the Three Worlds of the celestial, psychic, and physical domains. Native lore links Mount Shasta to the celestial dimension of the Sky World and Crater Lake to the psychic dimension of the Underworld; and while all "places"

A postdiluvian cosmos
The circle connecting the three mountains of the Shasta

---

must participate in the physical dimension, it is curious that the physical form of Mount Mazama is in a sense absent.

The Cascade-Siskiyou Knot

Using a pair of compasses, it is possible to prove that the triangle of points recognized by the Shasta are in fact positioned upon a circle that may be drawn upon a map. This circle is an appropriate geometrical representation of the postdiluvian world familiar to, but not necessarily inhabited by, the Shasta (on facing page). This circle like any other has a center, and it is remarkable indeed that the center of the world established by the three mountains of the Shasta is positioned specifically in the Upper Bear Valley. With this in mind, it is easily understood why this region should have been valuable to the Shasta, even if a mountainous barrier separated the Shasta's northernmost band from the other three.

Where it forms the natural terminus of the Bear Valley, this mountainous barrier is in fact the place where the Siskiyou and Cascade ranges meet. The uniqueness of this place, expressed at least in part through its exemplary biodiversity, has recently led to the establishment of a Cascade-Siskiyou National Monument, though most of the lands comprising the monument are actually part of the Cascade Range. Two peaks dominate this meeting place that are in a sense emblematic of the two ranges they belong to. Mount Ashland is at the very eastern end of the Siskiyous and is the tallest of all the peaks in that range. Close by is the lava neck known as Pilot Rock, traditionally called "Standing Rock,"[33] that is among the oldest volcanic formations of the Cascade Range. From the opposite side of the valley, along an escarpment in the Cascade highlands, Mount Ashland and Pilot Rock each appear to be an equal distance from the observer. Given the foregoing relevance of geometry to our subject, it is worth examining the implications of this

---

[33] Jeff LaLande, *From Abbott Butte to Zimmerman Burn: A Place-name History and Gazetteer of the of the Rogue River National Forest*, Medford, 2001, page 9.

arrangement of three points formed by the two peaks and the point of observation in the Cascades.

By drawing a circle that connects these three points upon a map, some remarkable features present themselves. In general terms, the circle marks a mountainous enclosure for the valley, excepting its opening to the northwest. Even though the modern freeway crosses this mountainous barrier at the Siskiyou Summit, the crossing marks in fact the highest elevation along this principal route between Mexico and Canada. The circular enclosure includes the summit of Soda Mountain at the heart of the Cascade-Siskiyou National Monument, Wagner Butte above Ashland, as well as the prominent ridge of Grizzly Peak that faces the town. Looking more carefully at the positions of Mount Ashland and Pilot Rock (pictured at left), the arc between them

The "escarpment"

approximates one-fifth of the circumference, which invites a consideration of pentangular geometry. By completing a pentagram within the circle, we find that in addition to the points upon, or very near, Mount Ashland and Pilot Rock, the eastern point is positioned upon Chinquapin Mountain. Near the northernmost point and below the aforementioned escarpment that follows the circle's curve, there is a wetlands area that, while closed to the public, balances both the largest alkaline fen and acidic bog in all of Oregon. The remaining point of the pentagram is directed with the flow of Bear Creek where Poison Lake would be had it not been drained. As for the other mineral springs historically developed in the Bear Creek drainage, all are contained within the circle, and the circle even includes Colestin Soda Springs despite their location just over the Siskiyou Pass.

Marking the center of the circle is the distinctive horseshoe shape of Emigrant Lake. The lake is in fact a reservoir, and though it serves as a focus for the region's recreation, the significance of this location was formerly much greater. A modern dam holds back the headwaters that

Ancient Secrets of the Rogue Valley

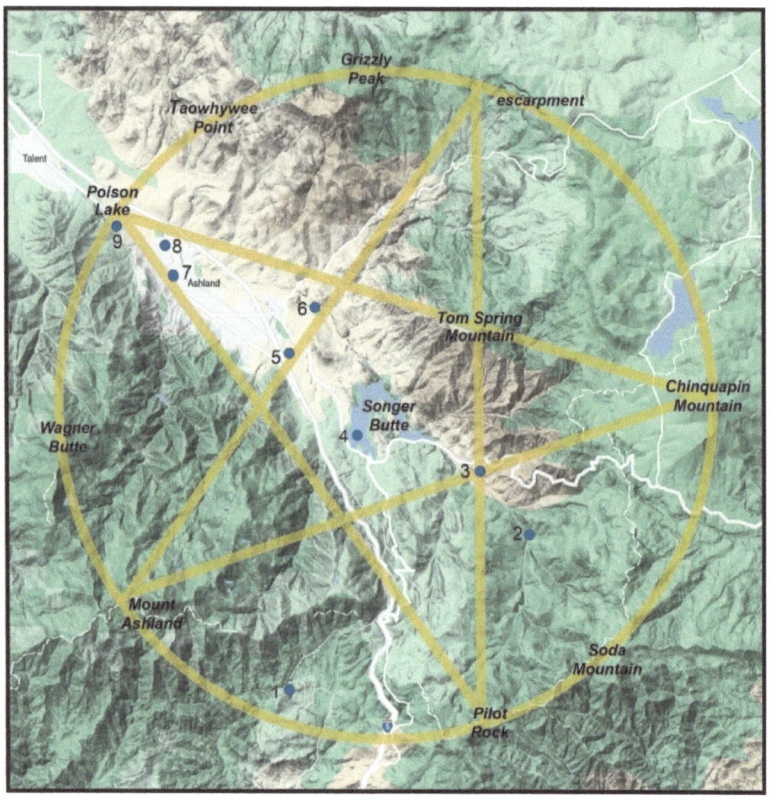

The Cascade-Siskiyou Knot
with historically developed mineral springs

1. Colestin Soda Springs
2. Buckhorn / Tolman Springs
3. Wagner Soda Springs
4. Kingsbury Soda Springs
5. sulphur spring
6. Lithia Soda Springs
7. White Sulphur Springs / Twin Plunges
8. Helman White Sulphur Baths
9. Jackson Hot Sulphur Springs

combine here, both from the slopes of Mount Ashland and, in the case of Emigrant Creek, from the base of Pilot Rock. Even after the creation of the reservoir, this place was known as Klamath Junction because two travel routes also met here: one road from the Klamath Basin to the east - the route followed by the Applegate Trail[34] - and another road from the Siskiyou Pass to the south. Before being inundated by the reservoir, the site selected for this junction was an artesian soda spring known as Kingsbury, and so this name was also applied to this junction. Two geologic formations also meet here, an older formation of softer stone and a volcanic formation, as they do elsewhere in the Rogue Valley; yet here, Songer Butte that rises above Kingsbury Springs and that marks the confluence of creeks has two peaks, respectively composed of these two types of stone. All these examples demonstrate a reconciliation between complementary terms, and such is characteristic of a place of harmony.

This attempt to identify a landscape pentagram is not entirely unprecedented; at the very least, it should not simply be dismissed as an artificial exercise. Indeed, it is well known that mathematical patterns repeat in nature, especially the mathematical proportion known as the Golden Ratio, and the pentagram is the clearest geometrical expression of this proportion.[35] Renaissance artists consciously utilized the Golden Ratio, or Golden Section, in their compositions. As for the pentagram, it has always been the quintessential symbol in Western civilization of a

---

[34] Where this route meets the circle are found the clear waters of Tub Springs, still flowing for the benefit of travelers.

[35] On the presence of the Golden Ratio and the pentagram in nature, see HRH The Prince of Wales with Tony Juniper and Ian Skelly, *Harmony: A New Way of Looking at Our World*, New York: HarperCollins, 2010, chapter 3.

harmonious constitution. In the ancient world, the Pythagoreans above all had particular regard for the pentagram, or pentalpha,[36] and would sometimes distribute the five Greek letters of the name "Hygeia" at its five points, with Hygeia being the Classical patron of health.[37] During the Middle Ages, the "Endless Knot" of the pentagram, or pentacle, was associated with Solomon. In more recent centuries the symbol was preserved within Freemasonry, an initiatory tradition that included Pythagoras and Solomon as its traditional founders.[38] The accommodation of pentangular geometry in this landscape is simply another expression of the Upper Bear Creek as a place of harmony, but the degree to which it conforms to this pattern is remarkable indeed.[39]

Among the first Americans to settle in the Rogue Valley was Thomas Smith, a practicing Freemason, who

---

[36] "Pentalpha" refers to the five alphas, or As, contained in its form; coincidentally, Mount Ashland is often called simply Mount A.

[37] Especially relevant to our subject is the long association of Hygeia with mineral springs; cf. the 18th century statue of Hygeia at Saint Bernard's Well in Edinburgh.

[38] René Guénon, *The King of the World*, Hillsdale: Sophia Perennis, 2001, page 11.

[39] Observe, for further examples, the positions of Tom Spring Mountain and Wagner Springs in relation to particular vertices of the pentagram, and so to the Golden Ratio. It is also of interest that a circle drawn around the pentagon at the center of the pentagram is very comparable in its area to the strangely unchanging surface area of Crater Lake.

established himself within the pentagon at the center of the landscape pentagram. His role as a leader of the settlers is challenging: while his relations with the last chief of *K'wakhakha* were respectful, if not always harmonious, Smith also served as a captain for the volunteers in the Rogue River Wars.[40] His funeral in 1892 was conducted by Ashland Freemasons, and the entire Ashland chapter of the Order of the Eastern Star was in attendance.[41] Smith is remembered as an active member of this first chapter, called Alpha, of the Order of the Eastern Star to be established in Southern Oregon. As its name indicates, the principal symbol of this order of elite Freemasons and their female relations is a pentagram. In a sense, their emblem represents a last vestige of Pythagoreanism in Christian America, although the five points of the pentagram are no longer associated with the letters of Hygeia's name, but rather with five figures from the

Emblem of the Order of the Eastern Star

---

[40] On Thomas Smith and the chief Tipsu Tyee, see Hannon, op. cit.
[41] *Ashland Tidings*, November 11, 1892.

Old Testament who are nevertheless female. Much has been made of a sinister meaning being attached to the inverted pentagram, and it must be admitted that a symbol's misuse allows its luminous significance to be replaced by a tenebrous one. While the Eastern Star is in fact an inverted pentagram, its Biblical anchoring in holy figures would seem to preclude such an interpretation, even if the reason for this inversion remains obscure. Likely meaningful in this regard is the fact that its central pentagon belongs to an upright pentagram that is unseen.

Of course, a society's use of a pentagram within the borders of a landscape pentagram does not prove a causal relationship, yet it is a coincidence serving to remind us that

The pentagram of earth[42]

---

[42] Detail from *Academie de l'espée* by Girard Thibault d'Anvers (1630), wherein is defined the "Mysterious Circle" of swordsmanship.

The Cascade-Siskiyou Knot

the symbolism involved relates also to the human domain. Indeed, it should probably be insisted that the pentagram concerns the human microcosm above any other expression, especially since the human form itself – with arms and legs outstretched - demonstrates the pentagram, a matter of key importance to Renaissance Hermeticists, as the example on the preceding page demonstrates.[43] There is a further coincidence to be observed here. As related elsewhere, the number five was of supreme importance for the traditional peoples of this specific region,[44] and the pentagram is obviously the geometric representation of this same number.

Although the geometry of the landscape ties together many complementary terms, in the largest terms it unites the Cascade and Siskiyou mountain ranges. For this reason, this cosmic pentagram might naturally be called the "Cascade-Siskiyou Knot."[45] As for its significance in human terms, this knot constitutes a setting for a succession of peoples, who, whether in the role of conqueror or conquered, are tied together by the landscape itself. However, the conquest of America signaled a change in how the landscape was understood. In the wake of the Gold Rush, the lands of the West were valued solely for their resources, and this was in keeping with the 19th century's increasing materialism and anti-traditional impetus. Even the historic development of the Bear Valley's mineral springs was in pursuit of

---

[43] On the microcosmic significance of the pentagram, and how the number five may be understood to be a number of Earth, see *The Great Triad* by René Guénon (Hillsdale: Sophia Perennis, 2001).

[44] Cf. *The Red and the White*, pages 73-4. The coincidence between this fact and the designation of the region's principal roadway, Interstate 5, may be noted.

[45] With less cause, the Cascade-Siskiyou region is sometimes referred to as the "Klamath Knot," after the popular book by David Rains Wallace of the same name, though the region so named by the author is not so carefully defined.

commercial interests. Despite the last vestiges of Pythagoreanism that originally focused above all on the fate of souls,[46] the traditional regard for unseen dimensions beyond the physical was being lost. Following the final departure of the last remaining representatives of Native tradition, the immigrants of European descent were themselves losing their own.

---

[46] The motto "FATAL" at the center of the pentagram of the Order of the Eastern Star likely relates to this aspect of Pythagoreanism. It nevertheless has an ominous connotation for those who failed to hold to the pacifism of Pythagoras, or indeed of Jesus.

3

Waters of Life and Death

The mineral springs in the Upper Bear Creek Valley form a chain of sorts, and the uppermost is Buckhorn Springs. As mentioned above, the traditional use of the springs was confirmed by two "crescent-shaped" mounds along Emigrant Creek, the largest tributary of Bear Creek. The lifeless bodies of small animals supposedly signaled to the earliest settlers the presence of the so-called "Poison Water," though it is much more likely that Native interest in the springs was clear enough to the newcomers and would have indicated the importance of the site. Captain Thomas Smith's contemporary General James Tolman was the first to develop the springs for commercial purposes, and so the site was officially known first as Tolman Springs. A bathhouse remains at the springs, though it is no longer used, and while soda water may still be drawn from a well and surfaces in the creek, the purpose of the bathhouse was specifically to make use of the carbon dioxide gas that is discharged with the soda water. It is important to understand how the historic use of these vapors was prefigured by its traditional use.

The principal account concerning the Native use of the springs in the Rogue Valley focuses upon the special sanctity of Buckhorn Springs. Its author C. B. Watson

The vapor bathhouse at Buckhorn Springs

includes a report of the methods of healing traditionally practiced there:

> Their method was to find a spot where the gas escaped, hollow out a sufficient space, spread fir boughs in it for comfort, place the patient on the boughs, where he remained under watchful care until he became unconscious. He was then taken into a "wiki-up", or tent made of skins and boughs and there put through a course of manipulation until he recovered consciousness. Then would follow a day or two of sweating and

> incantations by a medicine man. This treatment was continued until the patient was cured or declared incurable. All this time they drank the waters from the springs and used it for the vapor baths in their sweat house… The treatment was heroic, but the Indians insisted that it seldom failed to cure the most obstinate cases of rheumatism, asthma, kidney disease and stomach trouble.[47]

Watson claims that the springs attracted pilgrims from various tribes, and suggests that fighting was forbidden at the site because of its sanctity. While this last claim is an oft-repeated cliché attributed to Native tradition, it should be observed that the author's source was none other than Frank Riddle, a person uniquely qualified to transmit Native teachings from the Klamath Basin.[48] From this source, we must accept that Buckhorn Springs was visited by peoples of the Klamath Basin beyond the Cascade Mountains, and their return home at least suggests that fighting was not an unavoidable part of their experience. As for the sanctity of Buckhorn Springs, Watson relates his authority's report of Native belief:

> The people had a superstition about them and attributed their virtue to the "Great Spirit." The escaping gas was the breath of the "Great Spirit," and was a guarantee of a

---

[47] C.B. Watson, "The Indian Legend of the Springs," *Ashland Tidings*, volume XV number 47, 31 December 1914.

[48] Riddle had in fact been adopted by the Modocs because of his marriage to the heroic Toby Riddle, the so- called Winema or "Woman Chief."

sure cure if the patient had led a worthy life, but sure death if he had not. The place in which the "Great Spirit" chose to administer the benefits of his healing breath was considered sacred, and for ages was supervised by a great medicine man.

The earliest development of the site as Tolman Springs included facilities for taking "vapor baths." In the middle of the 20th century, ownership had passed to Dr. Herman Wexler, who operated a "sanitarium" for health at what had become known as Buckhorn Springs. Wexler was educated in Vienna, and utilized the vapor baths as part of a regimen to balance "Seven Life Requirements." At present, there remains the vapor bathhouse that contains six wooden boxes, with each providing an opening into the ground that recalls the Native hollowing out of a place to accommodate the patient. Each box allows a patient to sit directly above the level of the subterranean spring waters that discharge carbon dioxide, but with an opening for the head to remain above the level of the poisonous gas that settles near ground level. Clearly the loss of consciousness, whether supervised or not, was not part of this regimen.

Despite the unusual characteristics of Buckhorn Springs, it actually belongs to a category of sites recognized by Classical naturalists. Waters with noxious vapors were called *averni* (plural of *avernus*), after Lake Avernus near Cumae in Italy. In Roman lands, springs with potentially lethal vapors were often – but not always – incorporated into temples of Pluto, lord of the Underworld of the Dead. However, there is a spring in Anatolia with noxious vapors that should especially be compared with this American example. This spring belongs to the tomb complex of a saint known as Haydar Sultan. While there is evidence of earlier Roman use, the place now belongs to the tradition of Islam. The water in the well is cold and bubbling and drunk as at Buckhorn Springs, but it is above all the therapy of breathing its vapors that recalls the Native American practice, especially since unconsciousness may result from doing so. Indeed, in contrast to the vapor baths at Buckhorn, it is specifically the patient's head that is placed in the well at Haydar Sultan.

Despite the shrine's location in Western Asia, the spiritual current represented by Haydar Sultan appears to have its source in Central Asia, among the so-called "Masters of Wisdom" or Khwajagan. The saint is remembered as the son of the influential Khwaja Ahmed Yesevi.[49] Other inheritors of this Khwaja figure in spiritual lineages of the Ottoman era in Western Asia and Europe, in particular within the Bektashi Sufi Order founded by his disciple Hajji Bektash. Later, the Naqshbandi Order also brought the spirituality of the Khwajagan into China, and stories are even told of an alliance between Khwaja Afaq and the Dalai Lama in Tibet.[50] John G. Bennett helped introduce the Khwajagan to Western readers, presenting them as the heirs of an ancient wisdom that he even suspected to be Hyperborean in

---

[49] Alternatively, Haydar Sultan is conflated with the founder of the heterodox Haydari Order. Haydar ("Lion") is the namesake of `Ali, of the Family of the Prophet, and both Bektashi and Haydari lineages are distinguished by a special devotion to the Imam `Ali.

[50] Cf. Thierry Zarcone, "Sufism from Central Asia Among the Tibetans in the 16th-17th Centuries," *The Tibet Journal*, volume 20, number 3, Autumn 1995, pages 96-114.

origin.[51] In fact the Chinese borderlands of Central Asia is a region that has lately been offered as the likeliest candidate for the Classical understanding of Hyperborea. While ancient geographers posited Hyperborea beyond the limits of the Greek world (the name signifies "beyond the North Wind"), its people more essentially inhabited a lost Golden Age. The divine Apollo was thought to have lived among them periodically, and the development of his temples was attributed to them. [52]

When the ethnographer J.K. Crowfoot visited Haydar Sultan in 1900, there was much for him to report on. He requested of the Bektashi master of the shrine to be introduced to an old woman known as a "Sheikhin" (female guide) who served in a function that had been passed down always to a female. By inhaling the vapors from the well, the Sheikhin was able to deliver a message from the Unseen. After observing the delivering of the oracle, Crowfoot interprets his unusual experience as follows:

> I take the original idea implicit in it to be that there is a spirit in the well: to it the inquirer must introduce himself, hence I was obliged first to inhale the fumes; then the spirit is able to communicate his knowledge to a chosen prophetess, when she has reached a properly ecstatic condition: lastly, the spirit in question cannot be wholly dissociated

---

[51] John Bennet, *Masters of Wisdom*, Santa Fe: Bennet Books, 1995, page 35. On the Hyperboreans, see *The Red and the White*.
[52] On Apollo and the Hyperboreans, see chapter 2 of *Sacred Geography and the Paths of the Sun* (op. cit.).

The shrine of Haydar Sultan, like the traditional meeting halls of the Bektashi Order, has 12 sides (above).[53]

The meeting hall at Buckhorn Springs likewise has 12 sides (right); its groundbreaking was consecrated by a Tibetan Buddhist ceremony in 2003.

---

[53] As the number of zodiacal signs which the Sun visits in its yearly course, 12 is an essentially solar number.

from the occupant of the tomb.[54]

Crowfoot identifies the old woman as a "sibyl," and concludes that the methods at Haydar Sultan "have an exact analogy at Delphi" in the ancient world.[55] While it was traditionally understood that the vapors rising from a spring at Delphi enabled the Pythia to deliver her oracles from Apollo, the sibyl more precisely belongs to another of his temples, that of Cumae. In the *Aeneid*, it was with the help of the Cumaean Sibyl that Aeneas would descend alive into the Underworld from the shores of Lake Avernus. No doubt this association ensured that the "poison waters" of Lake Avernus were the most renowned in the ancient world.[56] Despite the association of these waters with the Underworld, it must be emphasized that Lake Avernus was not the location of a Ploutonion or temple of Pluto but rather a temple of Apollo.

As the "god of light," Apollo's solar associations are well known.[57] Along with its lifegiving power, however, the Sun also has a destructive aspect, as René Guénon has explained: "...the symbolism of the sun presents in itself the

---

[54] J.W. Crowfoot, "Survivals among the Kappadokian Kizilbash (Bektash)," *The Journal of the Anthropological Institute of Great Britain and Ireland*, 30, 1900.

[55] In keeping with this analogy, a tomb of Apollo formerly existed at Delphi; cf. *Sacred Geography and the Paths of the Sun*, page 27.

[56] On the importance of the *Aeneid*'s sixth book and the motif of the labyrinth at the temple of Apollo, see "The Labyrinth of the Age of Gold" and "Some Remarks on the Mystery Walls" in *Guardians of the Heart* (op. cit.). Perhaps not too surprisingly, given their present ubiquity, there is also a stone labyrinth on the grounds of Buckhorn Springs.

[57] Given the meaning of the name Haydar, it is worth recalling the solar aspect of the symbolism of the lion.

Aeneas and the Sibyl, Lake Avernus
Joseph Mallord William Turner, c. 1798

two opposing aspects, life-giving and death-dealing, productive and destructive, as we have recently noted in connection with weapons that represent the 'solar ray.'" [58] In his form as Smintheus, Apollo could be the bringer as well as the dispeller of plagues. Swearing by "Apollo Healer, by Asclepius, by Hygeia" begins the Hippocratic Oath; but while the Staff of Asclepius displays but a single snake as an emblem of healing, the Caduceus given to Hermes by Apollo

---

[58] Cf. René Guénon, "The Symbolism of Horns," *Symbols of Sacred Science*, Hillsdale: Sophia Perennis, 2004: "In Greek, the very form of the name *Apollōn* is quite close to that of *Apollyon*, the 'destroyer' (cf. Rev. 9:11).

depicts a balance between that serpent and a poisonous one. Especially relevant to the present context, Guénon compares the "twofold power of production and destruction" with "the two phases of the universal 'exhalation' and 'inhalation,'"[59] which is clearly identical to "the breath of the 'Great Spirit'" ascribed by Native tradition to Buckhorn Springs. Guénon further reminds us that "Apollo is represented as the protector of water-springs (the Celtic *Borvo* was assimilated to him in this respect),"[60] and it is not without interest that Borvo, through the etymology of the name, was associated above all with "bubbling" waters; but if mineral springs belong to the healing aspect of Apollo, then certain "poison waters" or *averni* may very well be under his patronage also, albeit under a complementary aspect. The temple of Apollo at Lake Avernus testifies to this, at a meeting place of the living and the dead.

No doubt the purpose of Apollo's luminous patronage of a place was always to sanctify its power. The presence of a temple relates to the role of the *genius loci*, just as the Pythia at Delphi succeeded, in a sense, the monstrous Python.[61] At Haydar Sultan, the saint is so closely bound to the spring that local lore recalls his martyrdom within the well; and so the *genius loci* of the place "cannot be wholly dissociated from the occupant of the tomb." At Buckhorn Springs, the power of its medicine was wholly attributed to the Great Spirit. Native methods at Buckhorn Springs alternated between exposure to the gas and the drinking of the water, and while the former was only possible at the uppermost of the Bear Valley mineral springs, each spring in

---

[59] "Symbolic Weapons" in ibid.
[60] "The Symbolism of Horns," op. cit.
[61] On the renewal at Delphi, see *Sacred Geography and the Paths of the Sun*, chapter 2.

this chain would surely have been recognized for its special benefits.

In Europe, "taking the waters" at its mineral springs remains a resource for healing and is customarily prescribed by modern doctors. The unique mineral content and healing benefits of each spring water must be generally familiar to these doctors, even if the value of each water's specific composition – not to mention the role of each spring's *genius loci* – may be only dimly understood. Needless to say, the Bear Valley's mineral springs are neither understood nor utilized by modern science.[62] This is rather out of keeping with the Hippocratic Oath still honored in name by American doctors, since the Oath properly begins with the invocation to the Classical patron of mineral springs. According to Charles-André Gilis, the invocation to Apollo and Hygeia reveals the Hippocratic Oath to be "of Pythagorean inspiration:"

> This association with the Hyperborean god indicates that "health (*santé*)" must be understood here in the sense of a realization of harmony and primordial equilibrium. "To drink to health" evokes the original condition of humanity that makes it possible to obtain the "beverage of immortality."

---

[62] In relation to Ashland's signature Lithia Water, this failure is despite growing scientific evidence that higher levels of Lithium in drinking water boosts brain development and reduces mortality (cf. Anna Fels, "Should We All Take a Bit of Lithium?," *The New York Times*, 13 September 2014). The failure to fully recognize the benefits of Lithium, for example against dementia, even extends to alternative medicine, due to the use of near-toxic levels of Lithium in conventional psychopharmacology. The "primordiality" of Lithium is acknowledged even by modern science, since it is among the three elements traced to the origin of life at the "Big Bang."

> Harmony and equilibrium reflect in the microcosmic order the attributes of Peace and Justice...[63]

Just as the Pythagoreans invoked the name of Hygeia within the pentalpha, the medicinal springs associated with our landscape pentagram have always called people back to harmony and equilibrium; and just as the Cascade-Siskiyou Knot binds together so many complementary pairs, the "Poison Water" of Buckhorn Springs reconciles forces of life and death. In keeping with the attribute of Justice, the breath of the Great Spirit at the springs "was a guarantee of a sure cure if the patient had led a worthy life, but sure death if he had not." Since Peace and Justice are complementary attributes, C.B. Watson's reference to the absence of fighting at the springs now seems more profound. Regardless, the lack of peacefulness among the immigrants was a clear sign that Justice would soon be lacking from the landscape of springs that is the Cascade-Siskiyou Knot.

---

[63] Ibn Arabî, *Le Livre du Mîm, du Wâw et du Nûn*, presented by Charles-André Gilis, Beirut: Albouraq, 2002, page 21. The "Hyperborean god" is Apollo.

Waters of Life and Death

The wasteland at Lithia Springs
under Pompadour Bluff

"Green Springs" Petroglyph

An elongated and oriented cairn

4

Sermons in Stones

There remain alongside the vapor bathhouse at Buckhorn Springs unobtrusive stone arrangements that may represent the flanks of a hollowed space that traditionally served to accommodate a patient. That there are two such arrangements suggest that they are synonymous with the two crescent-shaped mounds that were attributed in the 1970s to Native culture. Whether these arrangements do indeed belong to the latter, there is no doubt that stones generally provide the longest lasting evidence of ancient people. According to the Native view, the "Rock People" were the first storytellers: "The stories of the Rock People are so old that they survive in fragments...The memories of their stories are carved and painted on boulders and cliff faces."[64] The oldest petroglyphs in America have been dated to well over 10000 years before the present,[65] and they are less than 250 miles from the Rogue Valley.

---

[64] Doty, op. cit., page 69.
[65] Benson et al., "Dating North America's Oldest Petroglyphs, Winnemucca Lake Subbasin, Nevada," *Journal of Archaeological Science* 40 (2013), 4466-76.

Such antiquity very nearly approximates the aforementioned postdiluvian renewal, and concerning the expression "Rock People," it is certainly worth comparing this with the Classical legend of the flood. To repopulate the Earth, Deucalion and his wife were instructed to toss the "bones" of their "mother" over their shoulders, and understanding this to mean the rocks of the Earth, they did so, and people grew from the stones. Akin to the Native view, then, the Classical world understood "Rock People" to belong to the earliest of generations.[66]

While the age of petroglyphs may be approximated by modern science, it is more difficult to date stone arrangements. Most often arrangements appear in the form of piled stones or cairns, and based upon ethnographic data, scientists have offered distinct reasons for the construction of cairns throughout Native America. Sometimes surviving cairns are characterized as trail or territory markers; less explicable examples are grouped together as belonging to the "Vision Quest," and some have been habitually unrecognized.[67] A report on distinct forms of stone arrangements was undertaken by Joseph L. Chartkoff in "A Rock Feature Complex from Northwestern California,"[68] and it has the advantage of making reference to the practices of tribes still residing along the Klamath River. As a consequence, this study happens to be focused upon a region immediately adjacent to the circle of the Shasta cosmos, and this should be of benefit in evaluating the "rock features" of the Rogue Valley. This is especially important since these

---

[66] Cf. the "Stone Men" of John Layard, and above all the explanation of René Guénon in "The Cave and the Labyrinth" (*Symbols of Sacred Science*).

[67] See "Some Remarks on the Mystery Walls," op. cit.

[68] *American Antiquity*, volume 48, number 4, October 1983, pages 745-60.

Rogue Valley cairns are not only completely unknown to the general public, they have attracted remarkably little scientific attention.

In 1995, an archaeological report was prepared for the Pacific Gas Transmission Company as part of a pipeline reroute through the upper Bear Creek drainage. The report was deemed necessary due to the existence of cultural remains along this reroute, in particular at a site referred to by archaeologists as "Ridgeline Meadows." Since the report belongs to the gas company, precious little additional information has come to light concerning this site, aside from the very noteworthy discovery of a Clovis Point of the so-called Paleoindian period. However, an academic study of cairns in lands to the east of the Cascade Range mentions on the basis of "personal communication" that Ridgeline Meadows "contained more than 50 cairns constructed in the conical fashion."[69] This description is somewhat misleading, however, since a cone is circular at its base, whereas many of the cairns above Ashland are elongated in the horizontal dimension (see page 50).

In his report, Chartkoff found a comparable number of cairns in his study area: "28 on peaks, 32 on trails, and 3 obviously modern ones;" and observes that "the numbers of rocks comprising these cairns range from 6 to over 70, with an average of 14, most weighing 4 kg or less." There are many more than 50 cairns remaining in the Ashland vicinity, however, and while the numbers of rocks might be comparable in some cases, the Rogue Valley cairns are very

---

[69] Haynal, Patrick M., "The Influence of Sacred Rock Cairns and Prayer Seats on Modern Klamath and Modoc Religion and World View," *Journal of California and Great Basin Anthropology*, 22(2), University of California Merced, 2000, page 173. Given the context of ongoing development, the use of the past-tense "contained" here is troubling.

often comprised of many hundreds of rocks. Another contrasting characteristic of these cairns is that they are not found upon peaks and are usually concentrated in groups that would not serve as trail markers. Haynal includes the cairns of Ridgeline Meadows in his study of rock structures associated with the Vision Quest, but this assumption is inaccurate, and derives in part from his not having visited the site. The 28 cairns "on peaks" mentioned by Chartkoff might be properly understood in this context, but these cairns of the Rogue Valley are not upon peaks and too large for such a purpose. As for their age, the discovery of a Clovis Point among them should not be dismissed as irrelevant, especially in the absence of any conflicting data.

Without insisting on the comparison, there is an obvious superficial resemblance between these Rogue Valley cairns and the rock piles atop the so-called kurgans of the Central Asian steppe. Kurgans are in a general sense mortuary monuments, and the grouping of the Rogue Valley cairns obviously suggests the worldwide practice of interring the dead in zones apart from the living. Kurgans are sometimes arranged along north-south alignments, and there are arrangements in the Rogue Valley that demonstrate respect for the same axis.[70]

Kurgans, however, are essentially burial mounds of earth, and their stone summits are circular rather than elongated; yet elongated cairns especially suggest the shape of the human body. Significantly, the long axes of these cairns are often oriented to significant peaks on the horizon,

---

[70] Despite modern theories of Native migration from Asia that are at odds with Native tradition, this comparison needn't suggest "diffusionism." It might instead be offered that such comparisons are rooted in a shared Hyperborean influence, and this influence is indicated by the emphasis on the northern or polar dimension (cf. *The Red and the White*).

Rogue Valley cairn
(above)

Siberian kurgan
(right)

especially Mount Ashland. This characteristic in fact accords with Native funerary practices in Northern California: "Traditionally, when a Wintu person is buried, his/her orientation should be toward Mt. Shasta. Within Wintu territory, this generally would mean north. If a Wintu is interred in a non-Wintu area, then a proper burial would also be oriented toward Mt. Shasta, no matter what the direction."[71]

---

[71] Dorothea Theodoratus et al., "Statement of Findings, Native American Interview and Data Collection, Study of Mt. Shasta,

For the Shasta, the name of Mount Shasta was the same as the Creator.[72] For those who lived to the east of the Cascades in the Klamath Basin, Mount Shasta was the lodge of the creator and culture hero Gmukamps, "Old Man of the Ancients," who moreover had knowledge of the "paths of the Sun."[73] The greatest culture hero of the Takelma of the Rogue River was named Daldal, the dragonfly, who came up the river and was a slayer of monsters in ancient lore.[74] Strangely, the name Daldal also refers to a pair of brothers, as its doubled syllable seems to suggest. Since the younger Daldal is a trickster, he corresponds to the younger brother of Gmukamps who is called Was Gmukamps, or "Coyote Gmukamps."[75] Such similarities demonstrate that Daldal and Gmukamps are but formulations of the same figure. Edward Sapir describes the Takelma figure as "an amalgamation of the conception of the typical single culture hero, who is at the same time transformer and trickster…with that of the 'Hero Brothers.' The single culture

---

California, USDA, Shasta-Trinity National Forests," *Hearing Before the Select Committee on Indian Affairs, United States Senate*, Los Angeles: 12 November 1992, page 140.

[72] Theodoratus, op. cit., page 138.

[73] Cf. "The Modocs and a World's Heart, page 27. It is presumed that despite the title of his book *Life Amongst the Modocs*, Joaquin Miller lived among the Wintu, and so his analogous account of Mount Shasta as the dwelling of the Great Spirit should probably be attributed to them; on this account, see *The Red and the White*, pages 23-4.

[74] This function likewise belongs to Yi of Chinese legend and Apollo who slew the Python, and it may be noted that both were archers.

[75] Recall that Hermes sometimes appears as a trickster brother to Apollo. Cf. also *The Red and the White* (page 51-2) for personifications of the "double cosmic force" that corresponds to the *solve* and *coagula* of Hermeticism.

hero Daldal becomes split in two."[76] As with the example of Gmukamps, the memory of Daldal is attached to certain mountains, and according to the beliefs of the Takelma, Mount Ashland is not only the abode of this ancient hero but is the "physical transformation" of the hero himself.[77]

This does not establish that the cairns of the Rogue Valley must be attributed to the Takelma, since other people may very well have participated in the veneration of Mount Ashland. Indeed, the veneration of mountains is a practice shared worldwide, no doubt another legacy of the Primordial Tradition. More particularly, there is an association between mountains and the primordial human state. In the Chinese legends of the lands of the Eastern Sea, for example, the immortal inhabitants of the three mountain isles are called *xian*, a word interpreted to mean "human mountains." In a study of contemporary beliefs regarding Mount Shasta, Richard L. Tierney makes an important comparison between "America's Holy Mountain" and Muztagh Ata in the Pamir range of Central Asia.[78] Among Muslims, Muztagh Ata, the "Father of Ice Mountains," is also known as Hazret-i Musa, the "Presence of Moses," since the spirituality of Moses as well as of the Islamic hero saint `Ali are believed to be present there. [79] Unlike other examples

---

[76] *Takelma Texts*, Anthropological Publications, volume II, number 1, Philadelphia: University of Pennsylvania Museum, 1909, page 34.
[77] Jeffrey LaLande, op. cit., 1980, page 64. Alternatively, Daldal becomes the twin Table Rocks above the Rogue River, with the lower mesa identified with the trickster brother (cf. Doty, op. cit., page 66); the identification of Daldal with Mount Ashland likely reflects the beliefs of the Upland Takelma. Regardless, with its ability to transform, the dragonfly is an appropriate symbol here.
[78] "America's Mystical Mount Shasta," *Fate*, Highland Park: Clark Publishing, vol. 36, no. 8, issue 401, August 1983.
[79] It may be noted that Stern identifies a "Moses motif," albeit debased, in the lore of Gmukamps (op. cit., page 166). Concerning

from the Muslim world, however, where the spirituality of a place is usually embodied in a holy tomb, there is no known shrine upon Muztagh Ata since the mountain itself is the shrine. For this reason, Pamiri peoples "will bow in the morning when looking at the mountain, or recite peculiar prayers to call for his help and for healing, as if it was a saint's tomb...Thus, as a 'mountain-tomb,' the Muztagh Ata may be classified between the cults of deity-mountains and those of saints and grave veneration."[80] Throughout the Muslim world, pious people seek to be buried in the proximity of a saint's tomb, and it must be understood that for the faithful the owner of the tomb is not dead but rather "transformed" into the Unseen.[81]

The orientation of Native burials towards sacred peaks and the culture heroes associated with them is but a comparable expression of this practice, and the landscape of the Rogue Valley now appears to be a setting for it. Even if the cairns are but cenotaphs without actual human remains, there should be no doubt that they are expressions of devotion, and that their intended permanence testifies to an

---

Daldal, it is at least curious that the name the riding mule of `Ali is Duldul; the latter's dual nature is suggested by its descent from a horse and a donkey. In legendary accounts of 'Ali's exploits, Duldul flies through the air, and so the comparison with Daldal the dragonfly is not only phonetic.

[80] Thierry Zarcone, "Syncretism and the Superimposition of Islam on Buddhism in the Pamir," *Pilgrimage and Ambiguity: Sharing the Sacred*, edited by Hobart and Zarcone, Canon Pyon: Sean Kingston Publishing, 2017, pages 136 and 143. Zarcone's insistence upon the Muslim adoption of Buddhist beliefs is overstated, since there is an Islamic basis for the association of saints and mountains (cf. *The Red and the White*, page 50); besides, it is hardly surprising that spiritual communities would share comparable views on the nature of the same sacred place.

[81] Cf. *Qur'an* II, 154.

aspiration beyond the temporal. Obviously the traditional perspective differs markedly from the modern aspiration to "conquer" a mountain by reaching its summit; a traditional designation for Mount Shasta, for example, is "walk around and around, but never on top."[82] In a similar manner, the habit of naming mountains after ordinary people contrasts completely with, and indeed obscures, a peak's sacred identity.[83]

If the testimony of the cairns in the Rogue Valley remains all but unrecognized, much the same may be said regarding the region's Native "rock writing." For the late Thomas Doty, a local Native storyteller, petroglyphs and pictographs relate the stories of the "Rock People." Doty learned the language of the Rock People by traveling widely to sites that were rarely visited, and these visits required walking, or rather what Doty called "sauntering." For him, as for John Muir, "sauntering" meant to walk "*à la sainte terre*;" unlike Muir, however, the ancient writings were for Doty markers of the "holy land." His conviction that rock writing is a primordial language placed him at odds with the

---

[82] Theodoratus, op. cit., page 138.

[83] The grossest example of this is the sacred mountain now known as Mount Rushmore. For the Lakota who venerated it, the mountain was the place of the Six Grandfathers whose likenesses could even be seen in its stones. Obviously their images have been "defaced" by four others, and even though the faces now marring Mount Rushmore may have belonged to extraordinary people, it is very unlikely that they would have approved of what was done to that place.

official opinion that rock "art" merely expresses the whims of the individual "artist." It had always been assumed that rock writing could only be found along the Rogue River near the coast, but some 40 years ago a rock shelter of white stone was discovered in the Rogue Valley[84] that contained a collection of rock writings. Doty and his colleagues set out to decipher the markings at this sacred place high above the river, now known as Medicine Rock. Since the site remains inaccessible on private property, Doty oversaw the installation in 2008 of a replica of the marked stone at a local museum to help people understand this symbolic language.[85] Now, the Medicine Rock writings, like most of those on the volcanic rocks east of the Cascades, are painted pictographs rather than carved petroglyphs; and while these pictographs remain the only known example of Takelma rock writing, there are in fact petroglyphs in the Rogue Valley completely unlike the Takelma example.

Within the richness of his incomparable website, Doty has included images and, in one case, a brief description of a site containing mysterious petroglyphs that he was led to discover through personal investigation rather than academic research that is all but nonexistent. At the so-called "Green Springs Summit Campsite," Doty observed in the context of a cupped stone a "deeply incised petroglyph" (on page 50) that appears to be an example of what archaeologists call PCNs, or Pecked Curvilinear Nucleated

---

[84] This site is not far from the tourist attraction known as the "Oregon Vortex." Those most familiar with its mystery consider it to be authentic; the individual most educated on the matter, John Litster, maintained that another vortex exists "at the summit of the Siskiyou Mountains" (*The Oregon Vortex*, Gold Hill: The House of Mystery, 1960, page 4).

[85] Paris Achen, "Indian Pictograph Replica on Display," *Mail Tribune*, Medford, 17 October 2008. Doty was co-founder with Roy Phillips of the Reading the Rocks Project.

petroglyphs.[86] Since Doty's passing, our knowledge of these markings has grown considerably by the discovery of other examples in the Rogue Valley.

PCNs may appear circular or in various degrees of elongation, hence the term "curvilinear," with the central area or nucleus left raised, and so "nucleated." The proper recognition of this petroglyph type emerged only recently, beginning with a geologist's observation in 1972 that such marks atop California's Ring Mountain[87] were artificial rather than natural. PCNs had been noticed elsewhere, and had even been popularly thought to be hoofprints. In the case of Ring Mountain, the petroglyphs are now estimated to date from 5000 to 8000 years before the present, and attributed to Hokan or Penutian peoples who preceded the historic tribes of the San Francisco Bay Area.[88] The most thorough study of PCN petroglyphs remains a PhD dissertation by Donna Gillette focusing on the coastal mountain ranges of Northern California.[89] As indicated by a map included in the study (page 62), such a focus is warranted by the distribution of extant examples. It is also clear that despite the supposed Hokan identity of the Shasta, there have been no examples

---

[86] Elsewhere on his website, Doty sketches another set of petroglyphs he observed but did not photograph, and since they include circular elements as well as a crescent, they may easily be compared with the examples considered here.

[87] Despite the word "ring" that is a suitable description of a PCN, the mountain was not named for these marks but rather for a man named Ring, a revealing coincidence. It is also worth noting that a single cupped stone is still in evidence on the lower reaches of the mountain.

[88] Ginny Anderson, *Circling San Francisco Bay: A Pilgrimage to Wild and Sacred Places*, Lincoln: iUniverse, 2006.

[89] Donna Lee Gillette, *Cultural Markings on the Landscape: The PCN Pecked Nucleated Tradition in the Northern Coastal Ranges of California*, University of California, Berkeley, 2011.

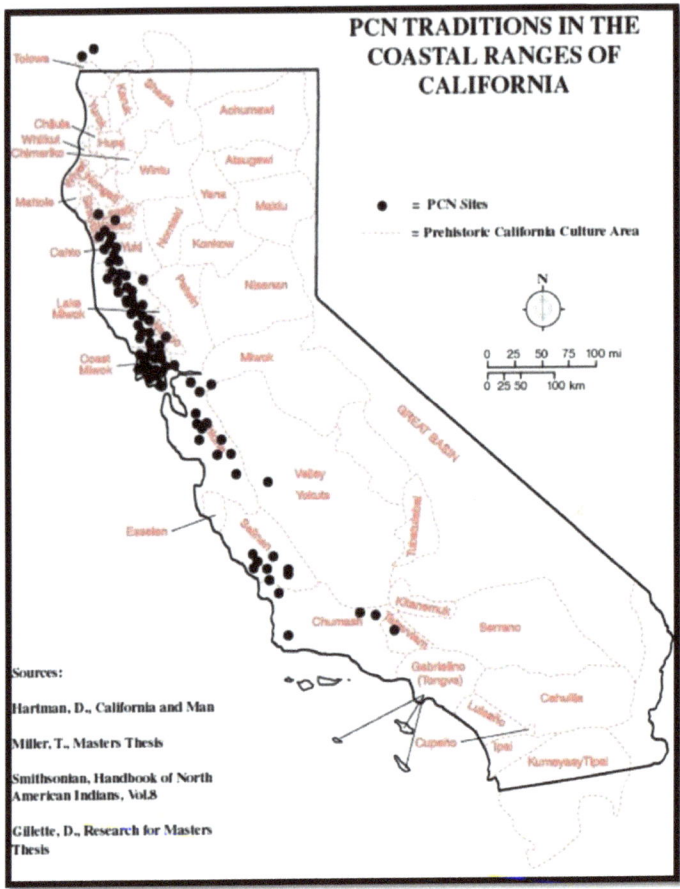

recorded in traditional Shasta territory; and even with the discoveries in the Rogue Valley, this remains true for lands indisputably associated with them. In the coastal ranges of California, there is evidence that the Pomo people in historic times believed in the power of PCNs to ensure fertility. Gillette supports the rather improbable view that the symbols represent female genitalia, but surely the possible benefit of the petroglyphs in ensuring fertility does not necessitate this interpretation. More likely, this persistent modern view betrays the "'preoccupations and cognitive biases of researchers.'"[90] In any case, the Pomo did not claim to be the authors of this rock writing: "The attribution of the PCN to mythic times implies that the Pomo informants living at the turn of the century did not claim direct authorship of the PCN and understood it to have arisen from a much deeper time."[91] For this reason, researchers should avoid limiting the significance of the marks to secondary "magical" benefits demanded by historic conditions.

It would be far better to make recourse to the science of symbolism, of which René Guénon remains the greatest authority. In a series of articles on the symbolism of the World Egg, Guénon offers insights that do much to illuminate the mystery of the PCNs. Obviously the ovoid form of this petroglyph type suggests the ovum or egg, but the prominent center clearly indicates what is truly important, that is, what the egg contains. In general terms, the symbol of the World Egg indicates the center from which a world's development will proceed; it therefore contains the seed or kernel of that world. Guénon very often made recourse to Hindu doctrines and Sanskrit in elucidating the universal language of symbols, and so used the term *Hiranyagarbha* or "Golden Embryo" for this kernel: "the very name *Hiranyagarbha* indeed characterizes it as a principle of an igneous nature; and this confirms yet again its central position, assimilating it symbolically to the Sun, which moreover is in all traditions alike one of the representations of the 'Heart of the World.'"[92]

---

[90] Ibid., page 44.
[91] Leigh Marymor, "'Baby Rocks' in Historic Pomo Territory (Lake and Mendocino Counties, California)," 25 November 2013.
[92] "The Heart and the World Egg," *Symbols of Sacred Science*.

Concerning the latter, we have already addressed its presence in Native rock writing with examples relating to Mount Shasta, including the pictograph pictured at left.[93] The splitting of the centers in these pictograph elements indicates a polarization that is part of the cosmogonic process, and it is likely from echoing this same process that "Daldal becomes split in two;" but we also considered the possibility that these elements represent geographic locations. Here we must observe that this split design is also found in a less common form of PCN that is nevertheless present in the Rogue Valley:

---

[93] See "The Modocs and a World's Heart."

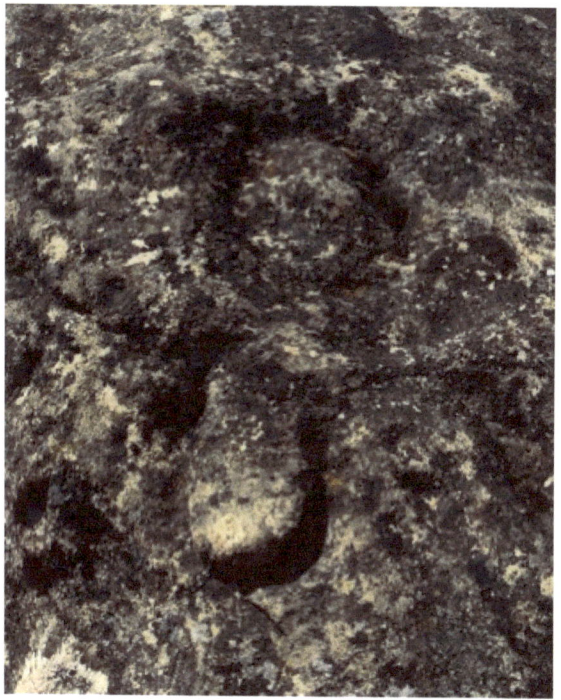

Rogue Valley PCNs [94]

---

[94] It should at least be noted that ancient Chinese characters for the Sun correspond well to these petroglyphs forms. The split glyph is equivalent to the so-called "small seal script" character of the Qin period, while the example on page 50 is equivalent to the character of the older, "large seal script," and it should be noted that this symbol for the Sun is found in East and West. However, since both these characters were used by the Qin, it is worth remembering that it was the Qin emperor who sent the court wizard Xu Fu to search for the immortal of Mount Penglai over the Eastern Sea (cf. *The Red and the White*, pages 71-2). Obviously the 3rd century BCE date of this expedition is not so remote as the supposed age of the PCNs. The motif of the rayed sun was a primary one in the arts of the Takelma; for examples, see pages 133, 141, and 157 of Earl Moore's unabashed

These petroglyphs along with others were discovered at a place where cairns are visible. Because of this, a relationship between the cairns of the Rogue Valley and these ancient petroglyphs should be considered. Now, there is no reason to reject the relevance of fertility to the petroglyphs under consideration, since it is not out of keeping with the symbolism of the World Egg; yet it would seem that such concerns are quite contrary to the purpose of mortuary monuments. However, it is essential to recall that any birth requires the end or "death" of the former state of being. No doubt this certainty informed the beliefs of the Pythagoreans regarding the yearly cycle of the cosmos. In the light of tradition, birth is not only into this world, and there are other births of an initiatic character completely unknown to the modern perspective. Guénon insists on an important distinction between two initiatic births, but leaving this subtlety aside, it is of extreme interest that these births are realized in the context of the cosmos as a sepulcher.[95] An association between "sepulchral" cairns and the ancient ovoid petroglyphs is therefore perfectly coherent, even when the former are cenotaphs.

There is still another contextual association to recognize: the ancient Clovis Point at Ridgeline Meadows was found amidst the cairns. For that matter, the Green Springs where the petroglyph described by Doty was discovered is the very location where another Clovis Point was found, and this area is included within the circle of the Cascade-Siskiyou Knot.[96] We have, then, a constellation of

---

account of his life of plunder, *Silent Arrows* (Paul Tremaine: Klamath Falls, 1980).
[95] See "The Cave and the World Egg" in *Symbols of Sacred Science*.
[96] Jack Meyer, "A Geoarchaeological Overview and Assessment of Northeast California," Cultural Resources Inventory of Caltrans District 2, Redding, 2013, page 125.

evidence all indicating cultural activity of very great antiquity. While Clovis Points have been taken from the ground, cairns and glyphs remain upon this chosen landscape, even if unknown. Of course, archaeology could only violate a cairn by excavating it, so there is some comfort in the general lack of interest, academic or otherwise; but there is no way of knowing what has already been obliterated. No matter the cause, such losses participate in the violence of genocide.

In terms of symbolism, there is a formal equivalence to be observed between the cairns of the Rogue Valley and its petroglyphs, since the piled stones of the former may be seen to correspond to the raised nuclei of the latter. As mentioned above, these nuclei suggest seeds or kernels, and it should not be overlooked that the words "cairn" and "kernel" both relate to the same linguistic root. René Guénon has explored the meanings of this root KRN in his study, "The Symbolism of Horns." As is clear from the word "corn" that is synonymous with "horn," this combination of letters relates to ideas of power and elevation. Most relevant to our subject here, Guénon addresses the formulation of Apollo as Karneios: "*Karneios* is the god of the *Karn*, that is, of the 'high place,' symbol of the sacred Mountain of the Pole, which amongst the Celts was represented either by the *tumulus* or by the *cairn* or pile of stones that has retained this name. Moreover, stone is often directly related to the cult of Apollo, as can be seen especially in the *Omphalos* of Delphi..."[97] In *Sacred Geography and the Paths of the Sun*, there was good reason to consider the symbolism of Delphi in some detail,[98]

---

[97] "The Symbolism of Horns," *Symbols of Sacred Science*.
[98] See especially chapter 2. It is worth noting that the Omphalos of Delphi was egg-shaped, not unlike the ovoid forms in stone being considered here.

and we must return to this symbolism if we are to discover what is indicated by the Cascade-Siskiyou Knot.

The "Horn of the Saddle" on Mount Ashland
These two prominent horns of rock recall the two aspects of Daldal.

5

The Solar Ray

Above all, we must return to the "path of the Sun" that passes through a number of Apollonian shrines in the sacred geography of Greece, including Delphi. This solar path aligns with sunrise on the winter solstice and sunset on the summer solstice, symbolized by the dolphin and the octopus respectively in Apollonian tradition. As the direct heirs to that tradition, the Pythagoreans believed the solstices to be gateways into and out of this world, with that of summer pertaining to deaths and rebirths and that of winter being reserved for the divine. We have already had occasion to mention the Pythagoreans, and it is worth insisting here that their doctrine concerning solstitial gateways is in perfect agreement with Native tradition.

Already I have addressed this agreement through examples specific to Mount Shasta,[99] and the landscape pentagram formulated in these pages must now be considered in light of this shared doctrine. Very remarkably, the direction indicated by the northwest point of the pentagram corresponds *exactly* to the azimuth of the

---

[99] See ibid., pages 105-8; cf. also "Racing Shadows" in *Guardians of the Heart*.

Ancient Secrets of the Rogue Valley

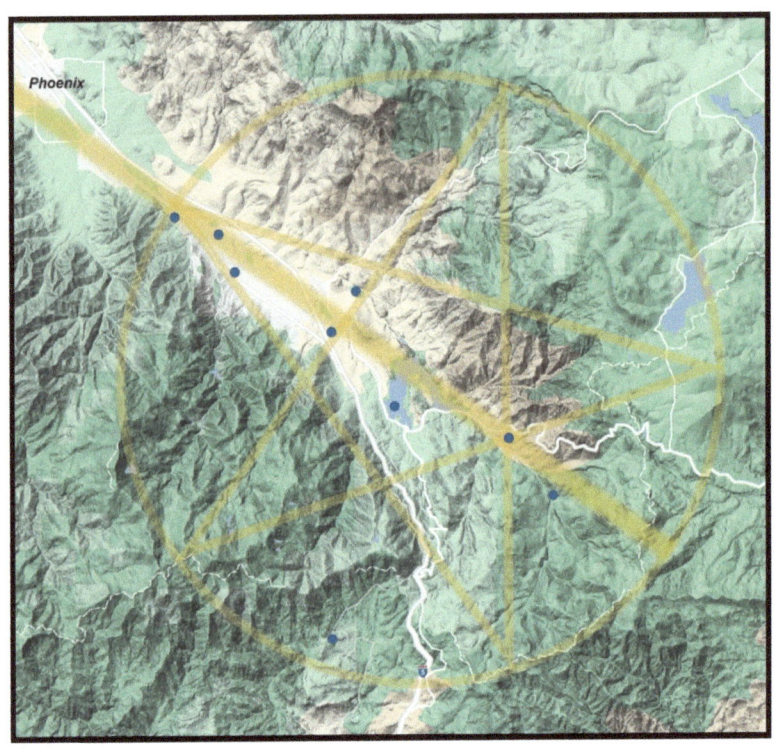

Path of the Sun
indicated by the azimuth of
the summer solstice sunset
(above)

"Ley" line
View towards Songer Butte
along the old route from
Phoenix (left)

setting Sun upon the summer solstice. This extremity has already been associated with the direction of Bear Creek's flow, and so it may even be maintained that the Upper Bear Creek Valley approximates a solstitial orientation, even if the alignment of the creek shifts further downstream. In a sense, then, every modern traveler in the Rogue Valley upon interstate 5, or upon the older highway 99, is following a "path of the Sun," at least in stages. Even if modern people are completely ignorant of this orientation, it must be admitted that Native people would not have been; after all, the function of "solstice observer" was integral to traditional life in the West, even in historic times.[100] Here is no doubt an example of the "topographical peculiarities that, far from being unimportant, have an incontestable symbolic value that must, in addition, correspond to those laws through which the 'spiritual influences' operate, which is a topic that properly belongs to the traditional science that one could call 'sacred geography.'"[101]

The Upper Bear Creek Valley is certainly not the only example of a Native landscape's natural conformity to the solstices. The same may be observed for the sacred landscape of Chaco Canyon in modern New Mexico, for example (see page 72). What is more, the length of that canyon compares quite closely with the Bear Valley, at least that portion of the valley that most nearly conforms to the solstitial alignment. Near the southeastern limit of Chaco Canyon, there is a sacred height called Fajada Butte that is famous for the so-called "Sun Dagger." This "dagger" is rather an axis of light that appears upon a circular

---

[100] Cf. Travis Hudson et al., "Solstice Observers and Observatories in Native California," *Journal of California and Great Basin Anthropology*, Merced: University of California, 1979.
[101] René Guénon, *The King of the World*, op. cit., page 25.

 petroglyph on the summer solstice; in its basic form, this design recalls the variant of the PCN that is divided through the center, only here the center is being actively split by a moving solar ray (at left). The extensive development of Chaco Canyon includes the laying out of mysterious "straight roads" that connect the site with significant places on the distant landscape. The clearest of these roads, the Great North Road, is in keeping with what has been dubbed the "Chaco Meridian," but

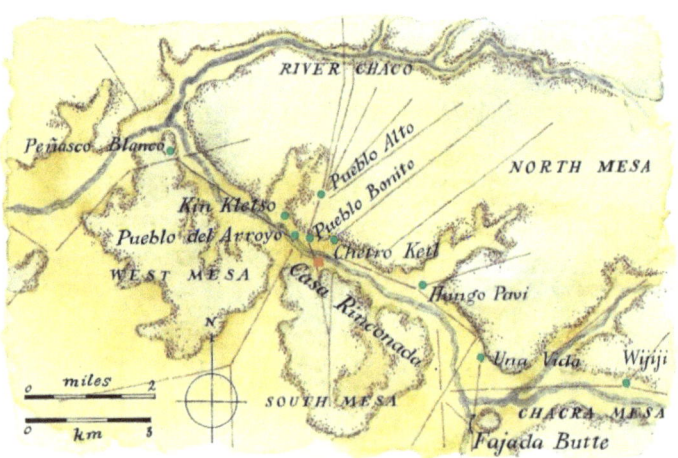

Chaco Canyon[102]

---

[102] Map from Geoffrey Cornelius and Paul Devereux, *The Secret Language of the Stars and Planets*, San Francisco: Chronicle Books, 1996, page 147.

The Solar Ray

which is really the north-south axis.[103] In some other cases, these roads correspond to astronomical azimuths.

Although the question of the rotated position of the Cascade-Siskiyou Knot was not previously addressed, it is clear that this position is not random once the positions of the Sun are taken into account. In this regard, it is useful to recall that the movement of the Sun throughout the year relates to the four directions of space. While east and west are marked clearly enough by the Sun's rising and setting on the equinoxes, the solstices represent the Sun's furthest displacement at its rising and setting to the north and south.[104] Now, it will be observed that one of the points of the landscape pentagram corresponds to a cardinal direction, and that is the eastern point; and while this orientation relates to the equinoxes, it should be insisted that there is a solstitial emphasis even here. Given the balanced position of the pentagram in relation to east and west, it is clear that just as the northwestern point of the pentagram is angled towards the north, its southwestern point must be angled towards the south by the same degree. For this reason, just as the northwestern point corresponds to the azimuth of the summer solstice sunset from the center of the figure, then the

---

[103] Just as this meridian connects Chaco to other distant shrines, the importance of the north-south axis was expressed by the Mound Builders. At Poverty Point, for example, its principal mound was constructed due north of the earlier Jackson Mound nearly two miles away.

[104] Cf. René Guénon, "The Exit from the Cave," *Symbols of Sacred Science*; elsewhere Guénon observes that the solstitial point of view has "a more 'primordial' character" than the equinoctial point of view (*The Great Triad*, op. cit., page 43). The solstices relate to a north-south axis, albeit in a kind of synthesis with the movements of the Sun. This may be compared to the authority of Apollo in the Classical world, since that authority had at the same time a solar expression and a Hyperborean or Northern origin.

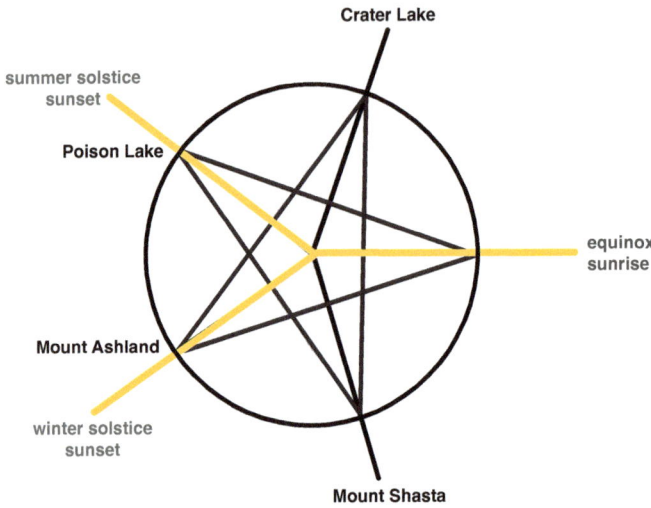

Alignments through the points of the pentagram
The "Pythagoric letter" Y relates to the solstitial gateways.[105]

southwestern point must relate to the azimuth of the *winter* solstice sunset from that same position.

That is not all. The remaining points of the pentagram, those towards the north and south, may be seen to indicate the locations of Crater Lake and Mount Shasta on the distant horizons. All the points of our figure, then, relate in a profound way to the Pythagorean symbolism mentioned above that is attached to the solstitial gateways. The gateway of the winter solstice is associated with the divine, and here

---

[105] Some have thought that Pythagoras himself introduced the letter to the Greek alphabet, and even Virgil is supposed to have authored an epigram to the letter Y; on its solstitial relevance, see René Guénon's "The Solstitial Symbolism of Janus" in *Symbols of Sacred Science*.

the winter solstice azimuth is directed towards the heights of Mount Ashland,[106] the transformation of Daldal; this is also the side of the pentagram defined by the location of Mount Shasta with its spiritual associations. On the other hand, the Underworld significance of Crater Lake defines the alternative gateway, that of the summer solstice; along its azimuth that leads directly past a poison lake,[107] the settled populations of the Rogue Valley are born, live, and pass on.

Besides the alignments proceeding from its points, extending the lines of the pentagram may be found to connect to other points of significance in the larger landscape. For example, the line running from Mount Ashland to the escarpment may be extended to Mount McLoughlin in the Cascade chain. The significance of this relationship should not be too quickly dismissed, given the Takelma understanding of Mount McLoughlin's origin: "Then Daldal set the mountain over to the east (from Takelma territory) and made him to be a mountain and tied him to earth so he could no longer move about."[108] Again because of the identification of Daldal with Mount Ashland, we find here a glimpse of an alignment's purpose, that of symbolically ensuring the stability of the Earth.[109] Of course, lines such as the one linking Mount Ashland and Mount McLaughlin exist only as abstractions; yet there are shorter linear cairn alignments in evidence that repeatedly conform

---

[106] Though the mountain appears mostly uninhabited, it has suffered from human development. For example, the "monstrous carbuncle" of a radar dome, as well as the scars of its ski slopes, are plainly visible from a great distance.

[107] Recall that for Aeneas, the path to the Underworld led past Lake Avernus.

[108] LaLande, op. cit., 1980, page 124.

[109] Of course, the designation of our pentagram as a "knot" is in keeping with this imagery of "tying" together features on the landscape (cf. chapter 5 of *The Red and the White*).

to the north-south axis, thereby suggesting a principle likewise demonstrated by the Chaco Meridian. Despite the evidence, the "straight roads" of Chaco are only dimly understood by modern science. The contemporary disregard for the Rogue Valley's ancient secrets is just another symptom of a stubborn condition.

There are nonetheless reminders of these secrets that because of their persistence are not easy to ignore. It was noted above that the location of the Lithia Springs has been despoiled by the region's gun range; but an archery club also meets there with far less impact, and so the association of Apollo with springs is here reinforced by the presence of archery that was among his principal emblems. In *Sacred Geography and the Paths of the Sun*, I explored the role of Mithras who in some measure succeeded Apollo in illuminating the paths of the Sun for ancient Rome, and like Apollo, Mithras was an archer. The iconography of Mithraism includes what is known as the "water miracle" that depicts the creation of a spring by means of an arrow from his bow. Despite the shared archery symbolism, Mithraic iconography did not include the dolphin and octopus of Apollonian tradition as emblems of the solstices; instead, the winter and summer solstices were represented by the torchbearers Cautes and Cautopates, with the former holding a torch upright and the latter a downturned torch.[110]

Now, as mentioned above, Lithia Water is still piped some three miles into Ashland from its source, and while it

---

[110] Op. cit., page 34.

was made available historically at myriad locations in elaborate glass fountains, only two locations still offer the water in more utilitarian fashion. Another fountain remains along the old route into town, however, that no longer provides water, and it is unique in that it is topped by a statue. This fountain displays the name Mickelson-Chapman,[111] after the woman who ordered its construction as a memorial. Her request specified only a "suitable life-sized statue,"[112] and a contemporary newspaper article quite erroneously described the latter as a "figure of a pioneer woman fashioned from Italian marble." [113]

In reality, the Italianate statue presents an emblem found in cemeteries, according to which the downturned torch relates to death; nevertheless, its origin must surely be in the Mithraic mysteries of Rome. No doubt both settings concern the posthumous fate of the soul, but this statue was never meant for a cemetery. Instead, with its statue displaying an iconography specific to the soul's journey on the summer solstice, the fountain was placed in 1929 upon a route that approximates the angle of the summer solstice sunset. In fact the statue's torch is aligned precisely towards that azimuth, with its flame going down like a setting Sun. Upon the plinth of the statue are inscribed the words, "They lighted the way," and no matter the reason for the inscription, it is especially applicable to this arcane interpretation. Is it a greater wonder that this iconography is

---

[111] The name Mickelson or Michaelson is significant in the context of the soul's journey, since Saint Michael was the psychopomp for Christendom (cf. *Sacred Geography and the Paths of the Sun*, chapter 3); the torch then recalls the archangel's flaming sword, and the word "brand" even applies to both a sword and a torch. It is also worth noting that the Mickelson-Chapman gravesite is immediately adjacent to that of Thomas Smith in the nearby Ashland Cemetery.
[112] *Ashland Tidings*, 14 April 1928.
[113] Ibid., 30 June 1931.

The Mickelson-Chapman Memorial Fountain

so openly displayed, or that no one questions its significance?

On 8 September 2020, the Rogue Valley suffered the devastation of the so-called Almeda Fire. The fast-moving blaze followed the course of the Bear Creek Greenway from Ashland and burned through the neighboring communities of Talent and Phoenix in succession. The fire was started under unknown circumstances at a place near Almeda Road, [114] about a mile from the Mickelson – Chapman Fountain but exactly north of its position. Curiously, the face of the fountain's statue happens to be turned directly to the north. In an ancient milieu, these aspects of the statue might together be reason enough to suspect that it serves a talismanic purpose; certainly the fountain no longer serves to dispense water. In any case, from its source the fire turned in one direction only, and its path (below) quite clearly conformed to that of the westering Sun on the summer solstice. While the name in Latin for the "Underworld gate" of the summer solstice was *janua inferni*, to modern people the word "inferno" means only fire.[115]

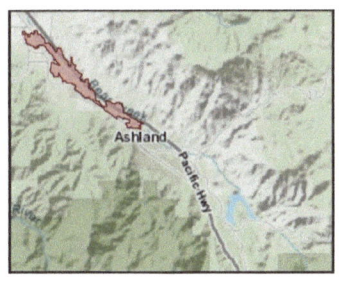

---

[114] As for the name "Almeda," it is not a variant of "alameda," a Spanish word for a pathway lined with trees, but in fact is the Spanish transliteration of the Arabic word *al-ma'ida*, meaning "the table." "Al-Ma'ida" is the name of the 5th chapter of the Holy Qur'an, in which the "table" is a miraculous one given to the followers of Jesus.

[115] The urban renewal project serving the needs of the Almeda Fire victims has been named "Gateway," and the "Gateway Site" is located directly upon the solstitial azimuth from the center of the Cascade-Siskiyou Knot.

It should be all too clear that in the context of fire and death and renewal, the participation of the name "Phoenix" is strangely appropriate here. The role of fire in the regeneration of the phoenix may be familiar, but it is not often recalled that this attribute of the phoenix was perpetuated by the legend of the Holy Grail: "By the power of that stone the phoenix burns to ashes, but the ashes give him life again."[116] What is more, from its earliest formulation, the phoenix has a solar aspect. Herodotus associates the phoenix with Heliopolis, the "City of the Sun," and describes its regeneration at the Temple of the Sun. We would do well to recall the "Golden Embryo" that was mentioned in the context of the Rogue Valley petroglyphs, since it was described as a "principle of an igneous nature" and assimilated to the Sun.

All this pertains to the "two opposing aspects, life-giving and death-dealing, productive and destructive" of the symbolism of the Sun. As emblems of the solar ray, the arrows of Apollo and of Mithras alike demonstrate both aspects.[117] The "water miracle" is an example of the beneficial aspect of Mithras' arrow. As for Apollo, Abaris the Hyperborean sage was his follower, and traditional accounts insist that Abaris traveled by means of an arrow; so here the

---

[116] Wolfram von Eschenbach, *Parzival*, Translated by Mustard and Passage, New York: Vintage Books, 1961, page 251.

[117] The bifurcated sword of `Ali is remembered not only as an instrument of death but also of life, since according to the traditional lore of the Battle of Khaybar, a spring rose up where his sword came down and struck the ground. 'Ali's ability to wield this sword is akin to his ability to ride Duldul, whose "dual" nature was noted above. Both examples demonstrate a power greater than that of the "double cosmic force" (cf. *Alchemy in Middle-earth: The Significance of J.R.R. Tolkien's The Lord of the Rings*, Temple of Justice Books, 2003, pages 9-10).

The Solar Ray

beneficial aspect of the solar ray is expressed through wondrous travel. No doubt the traditional use of the Bear Valley included traveling for its healing springs, and these springs are themselves arranged around the alignment that marks the last rays of the summer solstice sunset.[118] Modern people may still enjoy the convenience of wondrous travel upon this alignment, but local residents very recently experienced with the Almeda Fire a deadly power attached to the paths of the Sun.[119]

---

[118] The mystery of the solar ray in the Rogue Valley was in some measure caricatured by "Gold Ray," the name of the dam formerly at the far end of Bear Creek, especially since gold is the metal of the Sun.

[119] According to Chinese geomancy or Feng Shui, the danger of straight alignments is indicated by the term *sha chi* and the imagery of "poison arrows," which should no doubt be compared here with the position and terminology of Poison Lake.

Canoe with dragonfly emblem
Grandma Aggie's granddaughter consecrates a Native canoe in 2022 along the old route through Ashland.[120]

---

[120] Being displayed above dry ground so far from a river, the canoe serves as a reminder of travel along the "path of the Sun." The solar boat is well known from the Egyptian milieu, and even Helios, who drove a chariot, nevertheless had a golden cup that Heracles used as a boat in his Labors to reach the land of the sunset.

6

That Which is Lost

It bears repeating Martin Lings' insight that for Shakespeare, "just as for the ancient priests and priestesses at Delphi, Apollo is not the god of light but the Light of God."[121] The Delphic Oracle in fact participates directly in Shakespeare's play "A Winter's Tale," in which the audience is shown, albeit briefly, characters "quite overwhelmed by the blessedness of Apollo's temple, the solemn reverence of the priests, the unearthliness of the sacrifice, and the voice of the oracle that reduced the hearers to a feeling of nothingness," and so Lings observes that "Shakespeare is clearly determined that God shall preside over his play, despite puritanical laws to the contrary!"[122] The Oregon Shakespeare Festival remains the Rogue Valley's biggest attraction, but the Bard presides over the festival mostly in name; in 2022, for example, the festival presented half as

---

[121] Martin Lings, *The Sacred Art of Shakespeare*, Rochester: Inner Traditions, 1998, page 8.
[122] Ibid. page 161.

many of his plays as in previous years in order to give other shows greater importance.[123]

The message of the Delphic oracle is clearly stated in "A Winter's Tale:" "Hermione is chaster; Polixenes blameless; Camillo a true subject; Leontes a jealous tyrant; his innocent babe truly begotten; and the king shall live without an heir, if that which is lost be not found." The tyrant Leontes rebels against this divine warning, claiming truth as falsehood: "There is no truth at all i' th' oracle: The session shall proceed: this is mere falsehood."[124] What follows is the immediate death of the ruler's son and supposed death of Hermione, and it is the ruler's daughter who is "that which is lost." The daughter's name Perdita is the feminine form of "that which is lost" and is given by Apollo; according to Lings' esoteric commentary, "Perdita must be identified with what man lost at his Fall, his state of primordial perfection"[125] She first appears in the play as Flora ("flower"), personification of the Spring, and speaks of "things new-born."[126] To regain what he has lost, Leontes undergoes a penance of sixteen years that exceeds "A thousand knees Ten thousand years together, naked, fasting, Upon a barren mountain, and still winter in storm perpetual."[127] Because Leontes is so changed, he is finally reunited with his daughter who represents "the 'immortality' of primordial man which was lost and has now been found again."[128] Hermione is likewise restored, whose name is but a variant

---

[123] Not unrelated to this lapse, the festival has produced "A Winter's Tale" only once since 2006, an unusual hiatus in its history.
[124] Act III, scene 2.
[125] Op. cit., page 163.
[126] Act III, scene 3.
[127] Act III, scene 2.
[128] Lings, op. cit., page 166.

of Hermes, and who returns to Leontes in the final act as a statue that comes to life.

While Shakespeare had to remind the Christian world that penance involves fasting upon a mountain, the Native Vision Quest demanded exactly that.[129] Supporting Flora's importance to "A Winter's Tale" is bountiful floral imagery, and the imagery of flowers likewise invites comparison with Native tradition. "Flower Land" very often designates the paradisal higher world of traditional America,[130] and so this land is synonymous with the Abrahamic formulation of "what man lost at his Fall." In fact, in a perfectly preserved mosaic of the early Christian era, the phoenix is shown upon the Mountain of the Pole, and so precisely beyond the reach of fallen humanity; and this place is depicted in the mosaic as a land of flowers (see page 86).

In a previous essay,[131] I addressed the relationship between Mount Shasta and the Milky Way within the context of the latter being identified as a "pathway of spirits," but here it is worth recognizing that this pathway is also called the "Flowery Path."[132] What is more, the traditional understanding is that there is an earthly counterpart to this celestial path, and that it is precisely at the summer solstice that the "celestial and terrestrial routes are all so

---

[129] It might even be observed that fasting upon a mountain is at the origin of one of the pillars of Islam, the fast during the month of Ramadan when the Holy Qur'an was revealed.

[130] Cf. Peter Nabokov, *Where the Lightning Strikes: The Lives of American Indian Sacred Spaces*, New York: Penguin, 2007, pages 270-1.

[131] "Racing Shadows," op. cit.

[132] Theodoratus, op. cit., page 137.

Mosaic of the phoenix
The solar bird occupies the "high place" amongst flowers; the border of horned animals recalls Apollo Karneios, "whose symbolic connection with horned beasts has left traces down to this very day." In the Holy Qur'an, the "Lord of the Two Horns (*qarnayn*)" has authority over the paths of the Sun[133]

---

[133] Compare the bird atop the peak upon the figure's head in the "pentagram of Earth" on page 34. The quote is Guénon's from "The

congruent."[134] It is conceivable, then, that along the route of Bear Creek between Ashland and Phoenix is an earthly formulation of the "flowery path."

As for the condition of "primordial perfection" that Shakespeare's Perdita symbolizes and that must be found again, this is embodied in Native lore by the ancient white people, "a highly moral and civilized race" who were "the first possessors of the soil" in a "golden age of happiness."[135] For the Classical world, the Golden Age was a time of Everlasting Spring, and the Hyperboreans were its people. Hesiod ascribes a kind of immortality for the Hyperboreans since they live on as "guardians" over mankind, not unlike the immortals of Chinese tradition. A comparable conception is found among Native peoples, for whom the white people are hidden "immortals," and who, like the Hyperboreans, are recognized as the *genii loci* of certain sacred places. The Native anticipation of their reappearance corresponds to the cyclic return of the Golden Age according to Plato and others; Virgil describes this return in terms of the reign of Apollo.[136] René Guénon examined in detail throughout his works the Hindu doctrine of four ages (*yugas*) that corresponds to the Classical conception, and their place in the cyclic *Manvantara*. Islam offers a comparable doctrine, albeit for the smaller world of the Islamic era, since the Traditions include a prophecy that promises a sequence of four eras to follow the Holy Prophet, commencing with his

---

Symbolism of Horns;" on the authority of Dhul-Qarnayn, see *Sacred Geography and the Paths of the Sun*, chapter 10.

[134] E.C. Krupp, "Negotiating the Highwire of Heaven: The Milky Way and the Itinerary of the Soul," *Vistas in Astronomy*, volume 39, issue 4, 1995.

[135] Lucy Thompson, *To the American Indian: Reminiscences of a Yurok Woman*, 1916, pages 64.

[136] On Virgil's Fourth Eclogue, see "The Modocs and a World's Heart" and "The Labyrinth of the Age of Gold," op. cit.

Rightly-guided Caliphs, to be succeeded by commanders, then by kings, and finally by tyrants, after whom a Caliph will come again to restore a golden age.

No doubt the Gold Rush that precipitated genocide was a mockery of an age of gold, just as the immigrants of European descent were quite unlike the peaceful ancient white people, and whose arrival therefore parodied the latter's return. Such inversions recall the tyranny of Leontes in "A Winter's Tale," for whom the truth had become falsehood. Apollo's oracle had warned the tyrant that without restoring the proper order of things, he would be without a future. Make no mistake, the present condition of the Rogue Valley was accomplished by means of tyranny at once cultural and ecological. After all, these dimensions are really inseparable, as is demonstrated by the "human mountains," and as Shakespeare reminds us by presenting the character of Perdita as a flower of spring.

The creation of the Cascade-Siskiyou National Monument was an encouraging step towards healing the land from tyranny. It would be best for all the lands within the Cascade-Siskiyou Knot to be included in the monument, since its geometry defines an integrated whole; but even if that were so, a monument's status is still subject to governmental vacillation on environmental policy, and so private efforts are essential to prevent indiscriminate loss. Ironically, it was in large measure the rights of private property holders to be tyrants on their lands that has led, for example, to the present state of the mineral springs. After all, who but a tyrant would keep the healing found in mineral springs from others who might benefit?

Conservation efforts are being demonstrated at the Crest at Willow-Witt, a nonprofit organization educating the public through a private property in the Cascade highlands. Nearby is the EarthTeach Forest Park, likewise dedicated to education. Closer to the center of the pentagram, the Selberg Institute[137] has preserved much larger properties with limited public access since it is working to return the land to a balanced state, free of the burdens of the cattle industry; such methods help ensure that its cultural value will be protected and  that wild animals will be least disturbed. Most recently, the Southern Oregon Land Conservancy has acquired Pompadour Bluff near Lithia Springs and is supposedly aiming to open the landmark to the public.

Even the city of Ashland is poised to make a key contribution to conservation, following the purchase in 1996 of the "Imperatrice" property that comprises some 846 acres of rare open grassland. Unfortunately, however, the future of the property is by no means secure, and while unwise proposals for its development are still being considered,[138]

---

[137] This institute was named for fencing Master Charles Selberg, and we have already noted that the sword is to be included among the symbols of the solar ray.

[138] One such proposal calls for the installation of a "solar array" on the property, a matter of some irony here, and its pretense of providing alternative energy cannot excuse its lack of environmental sense.

the city literally fenced off the public in a deal to allow cattle grazing on the property. This policy ignores the ecological damage caused by cattle, and the challenge cows present to the resident elk population. Among the members of the public to be fenced out are representatives of conservation groups rightfully concerned for the survival of another of its native residents, the Grasshopper Sparrow. Official documentation conveniently fails to cite any cultural significance to the Imperatrice property.

Conservation is bound to be thwarted by a culture that is out of harmony with nature. The memory of Native presence on the land is given lip-service at the Oregon Shakespeare Festival and elsewhere, through the gesture of "land-recognition" that is in keeping with a wider trend. In the wake of the Rogue River Wars, however, gestures do not amount to penance; and while reminders may very well help transform public consciousness, real understanding is not guaranteed. For example, a key route into the Cascade highlands from the Rogue Valley is called Dead Indian Memorial Road, with the addition of the word "memorial" dating only to 1993. There have been more recent steps taken to change the name of the road, in keeping with the decision to rename natural features in the vicinity that had likewise been called "Dead Indian." These natural features are now designated "Latgawa," after a word of the Takelma people; yet this name properly belonged to a village of their warlike rivals nowhere near the present road, and is a name that means "knife in belly."[139] Replacing a brutally honest historical reminder with a somewhat arbitrary name that still means "dead Indian" is rather roguish, after all.

---

[139] Dennis J. Gray, *The Takelma and Their Athabascan Neighbors: A New Ethnographic Synthesis for the Upper Rogue River Area of Southwestern Oregon*, University of Oregon Anthropological Papers, number 37, 1987, page 73.

That Which is Lost

Far better was the recent naming of a hill near Ashland that is positioned directly upon the circle of the Cascade-Siskiyou Knot. The name chosen for this unobtrusive point is Taowhywee, after a medicine woman of the Takelma. Much more importantly, the naming in 2008 involved the participation of another Taowhywee, her great granddaughter Agnes Baker Pilgrim.[140]

More than anyone, Pilgrim gently awakened an awareness of Native tradition in the Rogue Valley. She was a beloved elder of the Siletz tribe who relocated to the lands of her Takelma ancestors, and though she was best known as Grandma Aggie, she also had an initiatory name relating to the dragonfly that was moreover the source of her totem.[141] In her last years, she attracted the attention of modern people in an unprecedented way to offer them traditional wisdom, especially on the importance of water. As the leader of the International Council of Thirteen Grandmothers, Pilgrim traveled widely and met with the Dalai Lama and other world leaders. Locally she was involved in many efforts to restore a Native presence, such as the installation of the "We are Here" sculptures in Ashland beginning in 2006. The sculptures include totemic depictions of a Takelma woman and Shasta man, and though Pilgrim was in fact the model for the former, she actually represented a much larger Native

---

[140] Pilgrim described seeing five eagles when she visited the hill (*Grandma Says: Wake Up World!*, Ashland: Blackstone Publishing, 2015); not only is the number five significant in the context of the landscape pentagram, but the eagle is, along with the lion, the solar animal *par excellence*.

[141] The symbolism of the dragonfly belongs especially to cultures east and west of the Pacific; Japan, for example, is traditionally known as "Dragonfly Island," since according to legend, the First Emperor perceived the archipelago from a mountaintop in this form. Recall that the Table Rocks of the Rogue Valley were perceived by the Takelma as dragonfly brothers.

world. Her husband Grant Pilgrim belonged to the Yurok people,[142] and her family after her has honored this affiliation.

Pilgrim led efforts to restore the Sacred Salmon Ceremony in Southern Oregon alongside her husband before his passing, and this led to its return to a traditional site on the Rogue River in 2007. Thomas Doty was a close friend of Grandma Aggie who, with his knowledge of tradition, assisted in the rediscovery of the stone "Story Chair" at this site. The installation of Pilgrim at age 87 upon the Story Chair amidst the river rapids brought to completion the renewal of ritual at the site after an interruption of more than a century.[143] Unfortunately, with her death in 2019 at the age of 95, the traditional use of the Story Chair has again been interrupted.

Thomas Doty passed away in 2020 due to an unfortunate accident, less than a year after her passing. No matter the circumstances, Doty's function was in a real sense attached to Pilgrim's. Just as she was able to address Native and non-Native alike, Doty's ancestry was both Native and British, akin to the Rogue Valley's history, and his understanding of traditional lore included both of these heritages. When Blackstone published a volume of Pilgrim's teachings as part of "The Legacy of the First Nations, Voices of a Generation" series, it was followed by a volume of Doty's stories. While the name "Pilgrim" was clearly expressed by Taowhywee's travels, it should not be

---

[142] On the Yuroks and their special relationship with the ancient white people, see *The Red and the White*.

[143] There is at this site an informational plaque with the heading "The Sword in the Storytelling Chair," and regardless of the details, the Arthurian reference is well-suited to the present context. In a sense, the Story Chair of the salmon ritual is a "throne" for a "Fisher King," and only the Grail can select that king's healer and successor.

overlooked that Doty's "sauntering" was really the vocation of a pilgrim.

Thomas Doty and Agnes Baker Pilgrim in 2019[144]

---

[144] Within months of the taking of this photograph they would both be gone. Although she passed away in the Rogue Valley, Pilgrim's remains were transferred to a grave on the Siletz Reservation in Northern Oregon.

Taowhywee Point

7

The Morning Star

Clearly it is worth considering the particular significance of the name Taowhywee, since it is the name of two Elders that has been transformed into the name of a hill. Taowhywee means "Morning Star," and so refers to the planet Venus in the sky before the sunrise. In the Pythagorean work *Harmony* by His Royal Highness (and now His Majesty) Charles, a curious example of sacred geometry specific to Venus is reproduced from the work of John Martineau, of the Prince's School of Traditional Arts. It depicts the wanderings of the planet in relation to the Earth, and the shape formed at its center is five-fold:

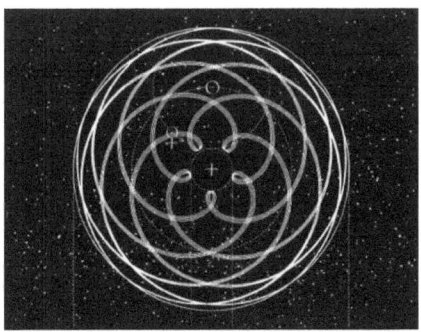

Yet as His Majesty observes, the shape quite clearly suggests the petals of a flower.[145]

Here, then, is a reminder of a principal teaching of Hermeticism, in fact the first teaching upon the so-called "Emerald Tablet" that describes a "work of the Sun:" "In truth certainly and without doubt, whatever is below is like that which is above, and whatever is above is like that which is below, to accomplish the miracles of one thing."[146] In relation to Venus, the flowers of the earth below are in some manner like the path of the planet in the sky above. In the present context, since the pentagram is the most common symbol used to represent a star, the landscape pentagram establishes a star upon the earth below. A further and very specific connection to our subject may be identified again in Hermeticism, according to which the alchemical principle of "white sulphur" is sometimes called "starry earth," as in the title of the early work by Ibn Umayl of Egypt, "The Silvery Water and the Starry Earth."[147] In the Rogue Valley, our landscape pentagram encompasses a number of "white sulphur springs," as we have seen.

Earth and water are also brought together with the star in the iconography of the Tarot, specifically in card 17 of the Major Arcana that is called "The Star." Even though the star is formed of eight points in the so-called "Rider-Waite Deck" of the Tarot that is the most well-known, there are other earlier examples in which the star is a pentagram. In

---

[145] Op. cit., page 116. In this context, it is remarkable indeed that the Arabic root z-h-r that signifies radiant splendor forms both the word for "flower" (*zahra*) and the name for Venus (*Zuhara*).

[146] Titus Burckhardt, *Alchemy: Science of the Cosmos, Science of the Soul*, translated by William Stoddart, Longmead: Element Books, 1986, page 196.

[147] *al-Mā' al-waraqī wal-ard al-najmiyya* reached Christian Europe as the book of "Senor Zadith" called *Aurora Consurgens* or "Rising Sun."

any case, we see at right a water bearer with her foot upon a spring, only the source of the spring, as well as of the flowery land's nourishment, would seem to be the water bearer herself; and this figure in some manner is related to the star. At the very least, it may be offered that the importance of spring water to the star of the Tarot is akin to the importance of the Bear Valley's springs to the star of the Cascade-Siskiyou Knot.[148]

THE STAR.

    Grandma Aggie referred to death as a journey to join the "Star People," and this is in keeping with traditional doctrines alluded to earlier concerning the Milky Way. She often referred to the "Old Ones" or "Ancient Ones" in a manner recalling the Classical conception of the Hyperboreans of the Golden Age. We have seen that the Native use of the Rogue Valley's healing springs is comparable to Apollonian tradition, while its ancient cairns

---

[148] In the Celtic tradition, a patroness of healing springs is sometimes paired with Apollo Borvo, and her name Sirona is from a root that means "star."

relate to the symbolism of Apollo Karneios.[149] For that matter, the former name of Ashland, "Where the Crow Lights," specifically invokes one of the principal animal emblems of Apollo. Pythagoras was traditionally regarded as the "son of Apollo," and his followers preserved the doctrine of the solstices as gateways for souls, a doctrine likewise present in Native America; and while the "path of the Sun" in the environs of Ashland has gone unrecognized, we should remember that Grandma Aggie herself declared that "Ashland is a threshold,"[150] since a threshold belongs to a gateway.

All these examples of congruence between the ancient traditions of Europe and America are at the very least indications of the presence of the Primordial Tradition. More immediately, however, there are keys here for understanding the harmony between Native people and their legendary white brethren. Amongst these keys is certainly the Morning Star, for it is not only the emblem of a returning Native presence. It also served as the very emblem that guided Ashland's first white immigrants in the Order of the Eastern Star, since "Eastern Star" is but another name for the same celestial wanderer. The Morning Star is the symbol here that calls together Native and non-Native, and in the form of a landscape pentagram it marks the Rogue Valley as a place of harmony "in which the 'Great Spirit' chose to administer the benefits of his healing breath." Above all, it is the cosmic function of the Morning Star to stand at the

---

[149] In words quoted above, Guénon associates Karneios with the "Mountain of the Pole;" and in Arabic, the title *qutb* or "Pole" for supreme spiritual authorities has the numerical value of 111. It is at least worth noting that in her later years, Grandma Aggie bore the traditional facial tattoo called "111" because its 3 lines suggest this number.

[150] Pilgrim, op. cit.

threshold between darkness and the light of an approaching sunrise.¹⁵¹

Thomas Doty was a storehouse of traditional lore, and for many years he shared his stories and made his writings available. For his readers he would provide this introduction:

> …you will find stories and poems and essays written in a way as to allow you to feel an inkling of what it means to be Native, what it means to call a rock cairn the home of the Rock People – not just a pile of rocks – to call a place home and to know it as you know your own skin…It is my hope that my books be a pathway towards things Native, a beginning. Then if your own heart opens up and you hear the wind speak the words of the Old Time Rock People, toss these books aside and step lightly out of your old skin, and into the sacred.

In this manner, Doty reminded his readers of the need for traditional perception. In this he followed John Michell, whose emphasis on the need for the "primordial vision" to accompany the understanding of the Primordial Tradition was based upon Guénon's elucidation of the symbolism of

---

[151] The Morning Star is also considered to be the identity of "the piercing star" called Tariq in the chapter by that name in the Holy Qur'an. This name in turn appears at Gibraltar or the "Mountain of Tariq" (*jabal tariq*) that along with Morocco's Mountain of Moses forms an archetypal threshold, that of the Pillars of Hercules on the western border of the Mediterranean. "The Piercing Star" (*al-Najm al-thaqib*) is also among the traditional names of the Prophet Muhammad.

the Grail: "Together they may bring about the state of mind and perception which is appropriate to a golden age."[152]

The presence of this "primordial vision" may also be discovered in the legacy of Pythagoras, even if it is usually unrecognized, despite the well-known existence of this legacy within the Christian and Islamic worlds. The Carmelite order of Christian monasticism considers Pythagoras to be among its founders, no doubt in reference to his sanctified example at Mount Carmel in the Holy Land.[153] An encyclopedia of Pythagorean inspiration exercised a profound influence within the Islamic world, but its authors were mysteriously known only as the *Ikhwan as-safa'*, or "Brotherhood of Purity."[154] In both these examples, the legacy of Pythagoras is inseparable from a life of purity, and this certainly conforms to the characterization of Plato, for whom Pythagoras was above all a teacher of a way of life. Surely it is in the context of a life of purity that Hygeia was invoked by the Pythagoreans; after all, the word "hygiene"

---

[152] John Michell and Christine Rhone, *Twelve-Tribe Nations and the Science of Enchanting the Landscape,* London: Thames and Hudson Ltd., 1991, page 10. Michell cautions that the primordial vision without tradition "provides a fleeting sensation of no lasting benefit," and this recalls the modern use of psychoactive substances. At present, the owners of Buckhorn Springs are planning to use its extensive grounds as a setting for psychedelic mushroom treatments, without any particular regard for the traditional medicine offered by the springs.

[153] On the position of Mount Carmel upon the path of the Sun known as the "Axis of Saint Michael and of Apollo," see my *Sacred Geography and the Paths of the Sun*.

[154] The *Picatrix*, or *Ghayat al-hakim* ("The Goal of the Wise"), is a controversial book of Islamic occultism that was especially influential in Christendom. It identifies Venus as the planet corresponding to the religion of Islam, and concludes, remarkably enough, with "seven admonitions" of Pythagoras.

is derived from her name. While the word "Islam" is related to the Arabic word for "peacefulness," Islamic esoterism is popularly called Sufism, from the same word for purity that identified the mysterious authors of the Pythagorean encyclopedia. According to the Muslim philosophers called the *Ishraqiyyin*, or "People of the Sunrise," the development of Sufism involved a living "leaven of the Pythagoreans;" yet according to them, however, the true *Ishraqiyyin* were those who "pass beyond theoretical knowledge (`ilm sūri*) to effective realization or the 'knowledge of presence'" or of "witnessing" (`ilm hudūri or shuhūdi*).[155]

The perpetuation of knowledges belonging to the Pythagorean tradition - as well as the Hermetic tradition - within Islamic esoterism are proofs of the latter's role in preserving wisdoms from a more ancient era. More than this, the "primordiality" of Islamic esoterism itself accounts for the agreement we have glimpsed between its teachings and those of Native America, in particular with the examples of the vapor springs and the formulation of the "mountain-tomb."[156] Concerning the importance of water, a contemporary Sufi master offered a primordial teaching that was likewise the message of Grandma Aggie. These are the words of Shaykh Nazim al-Haqqani of the Naqshbandi Order:

> Allah is saying, "We gave life to everything with water."[157] The beginning of life is water. What a secret it is. He sent life into water. We should thank Allah for creating us as Muslim servants. And He honored us

---

[155] *A History of Muslim Philosophy*, volume 3, Wiesbaden: Otto Harrassowitz, 1963, pages 377.
[156] For more on this subject, see *The Red and the White*.
[157] *Qur'an*, XXI, 30.

> with Islam that we became ones using water the most. We are using water in every way. A body revives in contact with water. Drink water and also wash your body with it...Old doctors are saying to drink water in the morning before eating...And you can't hear a nicer glorification than the glorifying of water.[158]

The following is from the book of Pilgrim's teachings:

> Do it every morning when you get up. Thank the Creator that He gave you another day, plus you can have a glass of water there and have a drink and say, "Bless you for keeping me alive. Bless you for being in my body and in my tears and in my blood." Learn to be grateful for the water...Water is our first medicine...Think of the water when you drink it, every day. When you wash your hands, take a shower, cook, wash your clothes...So it is a crucial thing, a needed thing, for all life."[159]

---

[158] Transcription from the "Saltanat" website (see *Sacred Geography and the Paths of the Sun*, chapter 10). While the Naqshbandi Order in all its branches developed from the lineage of the Khwajagan of Central Asia, Shaykh Nazim's authority included multiple other orders, such as the Qadiri Order (see Shaykh Muhammad Hisham Kabbani, *The Naqshbandi Sufi Way*, Chicago: Kazi Publications, 1995).

[159] There is a distinction here between listening and speaking, and this may relate to the respective positions of Islam and the Native tradition in the temporal cycle.

The word for the health (*santé*) that may still be sought at the waters of mineral springs, like our use of "saunter," derives from the word for sanctity. No doubt such a state of being recalls the "original condition of humanity" that makes possible the "primordial vision." To perceive the Rogue Valley in the light of the Golden Age, however, is not to imagine a landscape of the past. At this moment, there is a great responsibility to guard what still remains of the ancient inheritance of the Rogue Valley, and so participate in replacing tyranny with Justice. The time of the Morning Star is the dawn, and it is bringing to light secrets that signal a rebirth synonymous with the rising of the Sun.[160] Balanced against the losses of history, such discoveries are also posing the question: "Must not everything be found again at the end of the *Manvantara*, to serve as a starting point for the elaboration of the future cycle?"[161]

---

[160] The seminal novel *Dune* includes Apollonian elements in support of an indigenous and ecological restoration, with the hero Paul ("-poll-") being the son of Leto and whose mouse emblem and Atreides name recall Apollo Smintheus specifically, and all being under the auspices of Islamic eschatology; cf. my *Mysteries of Dune: Sufism, Psychedelics, and the Prediction of Frank Herbert* (Temple of Justice Books, 2020).

[161] René Guénon, *Traditional Forms and Cosmic Cycles*, Hillsdale: Sophia Perennis, 2003, page 26.

Qadiri-Naqshbandi Sufi Emblem
The pentagram appears within a much larger circle in emblems of Ottoman Sufi orders. This example is properly termed a "flower" and belonged to an order with dual lineages.

Temple of Justice Books

by Mahmoud Shelton

*Alchemy in Middle-earth: The Significance of J.R.R. Tolkien's
The Lord of the Rings*
2003

*The Red and the White: Perspectives on America and the
Primordial Tradition*
2019

*Mysteries of Dune: Sufism, Psychedelics, and the Prediction of
Frank Herbert*
2020

Sacred Geography and the Paths of the Sun
2021

Guardians of the Heart: Essays on Sacred Geography
2022

The Nine Sisters of California
Paths of the Western Sun, volume II

www.ingramcontent.com/pod-product-compliance
Lightning Source LLC
Chambersburg PA
CBHW041259170426
43191CB00028B/62